BERNIDA

"A True Story That Can't Be True"

By Tom Ervin & Al Declercq

Bernida Stern—Photo by Marcin Chomiecki.

© 2012 By Tom Ervin & Al Declercq
All Rights Reserved

DEDICATION

We would like to dedicate the *Bernida* story to all of the people that made her comeback possible. Thank you to the previous owners that kept *Bernida* sailing rather than allowing her to rot away.

Thank you to Toby Murray for his vision that one day *Bernida* would sail again and his persistence in advancing his dream. Thank you to Bart Huthwaite and Emory Barnwell for starting the restoration of *Bernida*. Emory did a beautiful job of rebuilding *Bernida* and devoted two years of his life and all of his savings to *Bernida*.

Thank you to Andy Groh, Todd Jones, Dean Kuhn, David LaMere, Bob LaMere and Matthew Declercq who contributed substantially and worked tirelessly to get *Bernida* ready to race the 2012 Bayview Mackinac Race.

Thank you to Matthew Declercq, Fred Detwiler, Ward Detwiler, Ken Flaska and Connor Flaska for getting more out of *Bernida* during the race than anyone expected. This crew did a terrific job racing *Bernida* and was the key to her victory.

The biggest thank you goes to Sara Declercq. Sara never outwardly questioned the wisdom of our endeavor and supported our campaign from start to finish. Thanks Sara for encouraging us to pursue our dream. *Bernida*'s victory would not have been possible without all the little things you did to help the team.

—*Al*

TABLE OF CONTENTS

Introduction	**7**
The Early Years	**9**
The Missing Years	**19**
The Verifiable Years	**21**
The Comeback Years	**35**
Toby Murray "He found her"	36
Bart Huthwaite "He bought her"	44
Roman Emory Barnwell "He restored her"	49
Al Declercq "Preparation for 2012 Mackinac Race"	57
Al Declercq "2012 Bell's Beer Bayview Mackinac Race"	97
The 2012 Round the Island Race	**135**
The Michigan Maritime Museum	**139**

Bernida

INTRODUCTION

As our subtitle implies, this is a true story that is so unbelievable it can't be true. The fact is, however, that the telling of this tale is as factual as we could make it. We conducted many interviews and then asked each interviewee to verify the facts as their interviews were being recorded for this book.

This story would never have been realized without many amazing and unpredictable events which occurred over ninety one years. Although it is the story of *Bernida*, a wooden racing sloop and a remarkable journey in and out of oblivion, this story is really about passionate people who are devoted to the sport of yacht racing.

Whether or not you are a sailor, the *Bernida* saga reminds all of us once again of the values of hard work, determination, creative problem solving, personal courage and teamwork.

Another interesting topic of risk taking is implied in the story of Al Declercq's gamble that this old boat, once partially restored, could carry three fathers and sons safely up the length of Lake Huron for two days and two nights. Balancing the issue of risk was the exhaustive planning and precautions which attempted to pre-empt every possible threat to the crew's survival. After repeated sea trials under real racing conditions, corrections and further reinforcements were initiated that truly helped to mitigate the possible danger of such an undertaking.

We hope you have as much fun reading the *Bernida* story as we did in writing it.

—*Tom and Al*

THE EARLY YEARS
1921–1927

George Owen
"The Designer"

George Lawley & Sons
"The Builder"

Russell Pouliot
"The Skipper"

Robert Roadstrum
"The Eye Witness"

Bernida

GEORGE OWEN

George Owen was the man who designed *Bernida* for a repeat customer of his, Sydney Beggs. The boat's original name was *Ruweida III* and was designed for ocean racing off Marblehead, Massachusetts.

George Owen came from a yachting family which commissioned boats from the well known yacht building company, Herreshoff Manufacturing Company of Bristol, Rhode Island. In 1890, after completing high school, Owen enrolled at Massachusetts Institute of Technology. In the late 1880's, MIT's Department of Mechanical Engineering began offering courses in naval architecture and marine engineering. Although he took many marine and naval architecture courses, a degree in naval architecture was not available until after he graduated with a degree in mechanical engineering. Between 1898 and and 1901, he worked in the drafting department of Herreshoff. In addition to drafting, he worked on calculating hull weights for the America's Cup aspirant, *Constitution*.

After moving to Canada in 1901, Owen began designing sailboats. His third design was a 20' restricted class of YRA Lake Ontario named *Whirl*. From 1902 to 1903, he won 29 out of 30 races on *Whirl*. This season proved that he had exceptional racing skills in addition to being an outstanding yacht designer.

In 1904 he and his wife moved to Massachusetts and he took a design position in the Fore River Shipyard. About this time, designers were experimenting with N.G. Herreshoff's new Universal Rule yacht measurement formula. This rule gave birth to the J Class of America's Cup fame. Owen had great success designing winning yachts to this rule. In particular, his R, Q, P, N and M Class yachts were quite successful against the established designers' boats on both the Atlantic Ocean and the Great Lakes. *Bernida* was designed as an R Boat.

From 1907 to 1913, Owen turned out 24 yachts designed to the Universal Rule. In 1912, his P Class boat, *Mavoreen*, set a course record in the Chicago Mackinac Race. Owen's most successful and innovative design was his N Class, *Dorello*, in which he introduced a high aspect ratio stem head rig. *Dorello*'s rig was later adapted by Herreshoff on the NYYC 50's and NYYC 40s. In 1908, Yachting Magazine voted *Dorello* Boat of the Year. In three years of racing with Owens at the helm, she

Bernida Sail Plan—Photo by M.I.T.

won an incredible 58 of 62 races. Owen's record of winning yachts and his technical innovations clearly establish his place in the upper echelon of designers of the day. In 1915, he accepted an invitation to become an assistant professor of naval architecture at MIT, a position he would hold until retiring as a full professor in 1941. He trained a generation of men who became highly successful engineers and designers in a variety of fields.

GEORGE LAWLEY

Mr. Beggs continued to have Owen design other *Ruweida* boats with roman numerals as part of their names. In 1921, The George S. Lawley and Sons Shipbuilding Company of Neponset, MA, built *Ruweida III* (later to be renamed *Bernida*.) She was a 32' double planked sloop.

George Lawley was born to a family of shipbuilders living in London, England. After serving an apprenticeship in England, he moved his family to Massachusetts when he was 28 years old. He worked for Donald McKay, an East Boston designer, until 1866 when he and a partner opened The George Lawley Shipbuilding Company. When George's son joined the business, the company became George Lawley & Son Company.

They began building pleasure boats. They quickly established a reputation as a company that put perfection into every detail. By 1908, the company had built 800 ships, including two America's Cup winners, *Mayflower* and *Puritan*. In 1921 the *Guinevere* was built at the company's shipbuilding yard in Neponset, Massachusetts. It was the first yacht ever fitted with diesel engines.

The George Lawley & Son Company closed its doors for good in 1945. Its last great accomplishments before closing were the construction of over 100 Landing Craft Infantry Ships for use in WWI. Later, the Department of the Navy asked the company to design and build Landing Craft Support ships which would feature a shallow draft so they could approach beaches and provide substantial direct naval gunfire to cover the landing of infantrymen.

RUSSELL POULIOT

Russell Pouliot was the man who learned about a very fast R Boat racing off Marblehead Massachusetts, in 1924. He bought *Ruweida III*, brought her to Detroit and renamed her *Bernida*.

Russell's father, Joseph A. Pouliot, was a French Canadian brought up on the Isle D'Orleans in the St. Lawrence River, about eight miles east of the city of Quebec. In his early life, Joseph and his wife Emily moved to Detroit, Michigan and settled in the French section of town. Here they raised two daughters and three sons. Russell J. was the first born in 1896. His father farmed in the summer and built custom yachts in the winter. As a result, Russell received training in yacht design and building. Beyond high school, he had no formal training. Those who knew him said he was an 'artist' when it came to laying out a boat and building it.

Like so many talented people, he was a dreamer and sometimes not practical. He was poorly organized and not a good businessman. He would often go out of his way to help a friend with boat problems regardless of the time or expense involved. Many people felt that his ability and good works far outweighed his shortcomings.

Russell was more than a boat builder. He was an excellent racing skipper for many years and was much sought after as a crewman. As a member of Bayview Yacht Club, he sailed and

Bernida

won the first Port Huron to Mackinac Island Race in 1925 aboard *Bernida*. He is considered by some to be one of the founders of that annual racing event. He later built the famous boat, *Baccarat* in 1932 and went on to win Mackinac Races in 1933, 34, 35 and 36. This boat also won the Newport to Bermuda Race in the Class "B" division in 1934. She was so fast that there was serious talk in Detroit racing circles of banning her from races.

For many years following the Mackinac Races, Russell would sail down to Harbor Springs and Charlevoix on Lake Michigan. He was known to yachtsmen in those towns as a winning sailor and boat builder. It is thought that he was chosen to design a new one-design class for use in Charlevoix and Harbor Springs.

Unfortunately, in 1956, at the early age of 60, he died of cancer. As often before in his business career, he had run out of money. A real tribute to him came from the love and admiration of his friends at Bayview Yacht Club. When he died, they helped bury him and pay for his headstone which has the inscription, *Bernida*. He is buried in Richmond, Michigan not far from Mt. Clemens.

ROBERT ROADSTRUM

Robert (Bobby) Roadstrum was born April 16, 1908 and died June 30, 2009. Without his eyewitness account of the history of *Bernida* in the early years, the amazing story of this great racing yacht would never have been verifiable. Because he actually raced on *Bernida* and helped prepare her for the 1925 race, we have the details which give this story such wide appeal among sailors and non-sailors everywhere. This is the story of *Bernida*'s early years in Bob's own words:

Bernida

Bob Roadstrum.
Photo by Toby Murray.

I was a 16 year old kid, going to summer school and taking algebra. I sneaked away one weekend to race down in Detroit. We finished a wild race on Sunday afternoon and headed home because the wind appeared strong enough to get us back across the lake, but we ran out of air in the middle of Lake St Clair and lay out there all Sunday night and Monday morning. The boat belonged to Russ Pouliot, who was superintendent of the Belle Isle Boat and Engine Company. He started to moan about me missing my final Algebra exam and also about the fact that he was missing work at the pay rate of $35 a week.

He also mentioned that he and some other guys were talking about a race from Port Huron to Mackinac. The Port Huron Yacht Club would be a sponsor. That was the first time I heard about it. I was very enthusiastic and, up and down the river everyone became excited too.

Bernida

In the winter of 1924, the first Port Huron to Mackinac Race was planned to be held on July 25th of 1925. Also during that winter, different classes and clubs pertaining to navigation and other necessities got involved in shaping the race.

Only three of the boats to be entered in that race were genuine racing boats with double planking construction. These boats were raced every weekend during the season and were well maintained by their crews. They were in the R Boat class and were named BERNIDA, RASCAL and NEAGHA. During the winter of 1924, I helped get BERNIDA ready for the race. Whenever they needed help, I was there. When it came time for the race, however, they told me, "Bob, there is no place for you on this boat." I was, of course, very disappointed. I wanted to be as good a sailor as these men. I was a good man on a boat for a kid.

So, I paddled my canoe over to CALYPSO which was also being made ready for the race. She had a hard time getting a crew, so I joined CALYPSO. We had a crew of seven. C.C. Gmeiner was its owner and, in later years, he became quite a celebrity as a good sailor. I came aboard and immediately started sewing up a sail and correcting mistakes. She was a 48' wooden yawl which had been confiscated by the federal government for hauling booze from Canada to Detroit. These were prohibition years. Even though the first Port Huron to Mackinac Race started during prohibition, every boat that lined up on the starting line had booze aboard. I heard that C.C. bought her for $500 at a government auction. She was in such bad shape that none of her equipment was ready for any kind of sailing.

When we got to Port Huron the following July, the beer was flowing. Several of the sailors, who showed up for this race, had sailed in the Chicago to Mackinac Races, which began in 1904. With the exception of the three "R" class boats (BERNIDA, RASCAL and NEAGHA), the rest of the boats were clunkers. Our boats were nondescript and in no condition to go on a long overnight race across Lake Huron. If you owned a boat though, you were going to be in that race.

Twelve boats lined up on the starting line. They were the three "R" class boats, a cruising boat named SUEZ, which had the current commodore of Bayview Yacht Club aboard, and eight clunkers, including CALYPSO. The course to be used was today's Shore Course, which follows the eastern shoreline of the State of Michigan northward. Four boats finished the race. BERNIDA, owned and skippered by Russ Pouliot, was the winner with RASCAL and NEAGHA finishing as well. Because the weather had turned quite rough, SUEZ put in at Harbor Beach, a distance of about 70 miles north of Port Huron. She took off from Harbor Beach on Wednesday or Thursday, finishing the race on Friday as a gesture to the commodore.

Aboard CALYPSO, the boat became unglued from the start because we had cable clamps rather than the much preferred spliced rigging. These clamps kept slipping and sliding. Early on, I climbed the mast to check things out. We would try to fix them on the leeward side and then tack and try to tighten them on the other. The race started on Saturday morning and the weather began to build by seven or eight that night to 20 to 25 knots. That kind of breeze was no good for that boat. We had a crew of seven and three of the crew became seasick. Later, one of the guys told me to go below and check on the mizzen mast. The area I had to crawl through was so small and confining that I knew I was becoming seasick too. Another crew member also got sick, leaving only two who were not. Under these conditions,

Bernida

we turned the boat around at Harbor Beach and returned to Port Huron. My first experience in a Mackinac Race was over.

In all, I sailed in 49 Mackinac Races and was awarded nine medals. As in 1925, so many of the hard blown races hit the boats sailing the Shore Course with the wind out of the north, creating a beat. This was true in 1925, 1945 and 1955. These were really bad, bad races that separated the men from the boys. My last race was at the age of 77 in 1985. Again, we were hit by a big storm and I knew then that I had become too old for this race.

THE MISSING YEARS
1927 TO 1953

The fate of *Bernida* during these years is a mystery. We know that Russ Pouliot sold *Bernida* in 1927 and that she was entered in the 1927 Bayview Mackinac Race and won again. This was the last time that there is any verifiable information on her whereabouts until she turned up in 1953 on Lake Muskegon under the ownership of Austin Freye. Although numerous attempts have been made to trace the boat and its whereabouts prior to 1953, they have been in vain.

Bernida

Bernida

The Verifiable Years

"1953 to 1957"

Bernida reappeared on Lake Muskegon in 1953 under the ownership of Austin Freye, the manager of a local lumber yard. His son David remembers that his dad redecked the boat with special plywood. There were two other R Boats on Lake Muskegon during that period. He named the boat *Pirate*. He raced her locally and often won. Austin also built boats himself, so it can be assumed that, like Russ Pouliot, as a fellow boat builder, he recognized good racing design when he saw it. He sold the boat in 1957.

John Olwin, Family & Friends in Lake Michigan.
Photo by Barbara Alt.

Bernida

"1957 to 1975"

Dr. John Olwin (John) was driving north on Michigan State Road 31 in western Michigan in the summer of 1957 when he spotted an old wooden sailboat alongside the road with a For Sale sign. It was an instant love affair. He bought the boat and took her to Lake Pentwater where she would reside for the next 18 years. As daughter Barbara would later relate, "There can be no owner who loved that boat more than my father." He had a partner named Dr. Robinson. They took their last names, Olwin and Robinson, and named the boat, *OLROB*. Like Austin Freye before him, he had no idea that this boat had a remarkable history as a racing champion.

When Dr. Robinson and his wife moved to Africa, John got a new partner, Dr. Raymond Galt. Dr. Galt was actively involved with the boat for a while, but the great majority of time spent sailing aboard *Bernida* was by the Olwin family.

John taught horsemanship and sailing at Camp Charlevoix. He also taught at Culver Military Academy. He was a quintessential gentleman, very kind and gentle. His priorities in life were family, patients and sailing. His personality was very consistent except when he stepped aboard *OLROB*. He loved barking orders to the crew.

One of the more interesting events happened each summer when his nieces, Margie and Patty came to visit. They were both Benedictine nuns serving on the faculty of the College of St. Scholastica in Duluth, Minnesota. They wore the nuns' habits of that era with the long starched gowns that touched the floor. John was always delighted when the nuns came to visit because they were just as crazy about sailing as he was. Barb and her sister Holly recall the days with the nuns tacking up the Pentwater Channel to Lake Michigan and the nuns scurrying around the deck in their long flowing gowns flying in the breeze. Both Barb and Holly and their husbands had many years of fun on that sailboat. The deck was painted light blue with sand mixed into the paint giving them good footing. It had heavy canvas sails which had a slight scent of mildew. On January 8, 1975, after 18 fun filled years, John donated the boat to the Sea Explorers in Pentwater.

"1975 TO 1979"

Sea Explorer Ship 100 was the proud new owner of *Bernida*. It was owned by them until 1979 with two years spent sailing in Ludington and the last two years on Lake Pentwater. Dr. Richard Williams, a dentist in Pentwater, was the boat's skipper. It served many boys ages 11 to 16 during those years. They

Lake Pentwater Sea Explorer Ship 100—Photo by Dr. Richard Williams.

Bernida

called her the "death machine" because, when it got wild on Lake Michigan, the boat would submarine through the waves. The Sea Explorers sold the boat to Terry and Sammy Craig.

"1979 TO 1983"

Terry and Sammy Craig, local Pentwater residents, bought *Bernida* from the Sea Explorers and owned the boat until 1983. Sammy had been a frequent crew member when Dr. Olwin owned her and probably was happy to have her back as his boat. Numerous attempts have been made to contact the Craigs in order to learn of their experiences with the boat, but those efforts have not been successful.

"1983 TO 1996"

Jeff Spencer became the owner of *Bernida* quite by accident. In the fall of 1983, the boat really wasn't for sale at the time, but Jeff had a friend, John Shrauger, who loved sailing and wanted to buy *Bernida* from the Craigs. A sale price was agreed upon in the amount of $2,500. There was a snag before the purchase could go forward. Jeff had never been on a sailboat in his life, and was a bit uncertain about this partnership opportunity. Jeff had never thought about owning a sailboat, so John took him out on the boat for a one hour sail on Pentwater Lake. That did it! Jeff loved the boat and instantly loved sailing.

The sale closed in September of 1983. Jeff, who grew up on a fruit farm near Hart, Michigan was the type who liked to do his research before taking on a new enterprise. He bought books on sailing. He was also working in Grand Rapids and attending Michigan State University as a part time student in pursuit of an engineering degree.

Upon closer inspection after the purchase, it became obvious that the boat was going to need a lot of work. The decking was rotted, although it had been replaced once. The hatches were soft and the ribs were cracked at the waterline. John decided that he needed to dedicate all of his finances and time towards the pursuit of his education and career. So he sold his half interest in the boat to Jeff in November of that year. With this strange turn of events, Jeff, who didn't know anything about sailing other than what he was beginning to learn in books, was the dubious owner of a sixty two year old wooden boat in great need of restoration.

  His first decision as the new owner was to pull the boat out of the water for a year so that needed repairs could be completed. It had a rotted plywood deck, punky and soft-hatches, a stern with severe dry rot, and many cracked ribs. He called his high school woodshop teacher for advice and he found a guy who had done boat building. John's dad owned a lumber yard with a warehouse. It was here that Jeff stored the boat and worked on it 4 or 5 nights a week until midnight, after working at the family farm all day. John's dad charged him the meager amount of $200 a year to store his boat there. He would think about the boat during the day and decide what work he wanted to do on the boat that night. He bought some mahogany that he had seen in Wooden Boat magazine. He also used pressure treated plywood for the decking because marine plywood was too expensive. When he purchased the boat, all he knew was that it was a cool looking old sailboat. He had no idea that it had an impressive race history.

  For a number of years in the late 70s and early 80s, Pentwater was also home to an old wooden 12 Meter boat, the *Northern Light (US 14)*. Her racing crew was recruited from all over, including the Detroit area.

Northern Light Under Sail—Photo by Lane Dupont.

Northern Light was a gift to 24-year old Lee Loomis, Jr., from his father in 1938 as an incentive to keep his son from going off to Europe where war was imminent.

Twenty years later, she became the prized possession of the famous Greek shipping tycoon, Stavaros Niarchos. He renamed her *Nereus* and it was under this name that she participated in the America's Cup in 1958 as the trial horse for *Columbia*. In 1962, she saw cup service again and in 1964 worked with the American defense team and *Constellation*.

Eventually, *Northern Light* was purchased by Buckey Neasly and John Andre and taken to the Great Lakes where she cruised and raced successfully for years. Al Declercq was a junior in high school at that time and was part of the delivery crew that sailed *Northern Light* from Buffalo, NY to Detroit. She had several other owners before finally falling into disrepair and was abandoned in Holland, Michigan. She sat forlorn tied to a dock without paint, varnish or maintenance while the vandals picked

Bayview Yacht Club—Photo by Kerrie Barno.

Bernida

her clean. For years she struggled through the snow and ice of winter and the heat of the summer with two household cellar pumps running continuously to keep her afloat. She finally sank and was later restored by the late Bob Tiedemann.

   Some of the Detroit area crew on *Northern Light* saw Jeff's boat in Pentwater and suggested that she could be one of the famed R Class sloops that had been banned from the Port Huron race back in the 20s. This casual conversation completely altered the future of *Bernida*! With this information, Jeff started doing some research. He got an old Bayview Mackinac Race brochure that had sketches of the boats in the R-class fleet, and thought that the sketch of the *Bernida* looked like his boat. Next, he contacted the Bayview Yacht Club, and sent them some pictures to see if anyone could verify whether his boat was one of these original R Boats.

The yacht club put him in touch with Mr. Robert Roadstrum, and Bob put all the pieces together for him.

   On September 28, 1984, he wrote Jeff the following letter:
Dear Mr. Spencer,
Your letter and pictures received here at the Bayview Yacht Club September 21st were forwarded to me and came as a pleasant surprise. Yes, the old wooden boat you've recently purchased is indeed Bernida, the first boat to finish in Bayview's first Mackinac Race in 1925.

   When I was a youngster I sailed aboard that boat as a junior crew. Russ Pouliot owned her then. His younger brother Carl and I were the "go-fer" kids helping Russ build a water tight cockpit in her. When Bernida came to Detroit in 1925, Pouliot intended racing her in the proposed Bayview Mackinac race. In order to do so he had to add a water tight or self bailing cockpit. Your boat had a water tight cockpit but would not drain because the bottom of the cockpit was below the waterline.

She was built in 1921 at the George Lawley & Sons yard in Boston for, as I recall, a man by the name of Sydney A. Beggs. Her original name was Ruweida III. George Owen, a professor of marine architecture at the Massachusetts Institute of Technology (M.I.T.) designed her as he did all of Mr. Beggs' boats. Professor Owen was a true innovator and one of the leading yacht designers of his day. Many of the most successful "R", "Q" and "P" boats all built to the Universal Rule as racing yachts came from his board. Most of the great "R" boats sailed out of Marblehead, Mass. as did your boat. To save weight, most had deep open cockpits.

Here are the specs for your boat:

Original owner:	Sydney A. Beggs
"R" Class yacht name:	Ruweida III, Sail# R 38
Home port:	Marblehead, Mass.
Designer:	Prof. George Owen, M.I.T.
Builder:	George Lawley & Sons
L.O.A.:	32'2"
L.W.L.:	23'6"
Beam:	8'
Original draft:	5'5"
Displacement:	9,300 lbs.
Sail Area:	600 sqft.

Renamed Bernida in 1925 by Russell J. Pouliot

The information regarding Bernida's dimensions was given to me by Professor Owen at the time he presented Bayview Yacht Club with the half model of the boat.

Going back to 1925 where this story starts, Russ Pouliot a local boat designer and builder, teamed up with Neil Lynch, a stock broker here in Detroit, to buy two "R" boats from the

Bernida

Marblehead fleet, to bolster the then blossoming fleet of "R"s in this area. Russ bought Ruweida III and Lynch bought Lightning. Ruweida had been a more or less, in and outer. On the other hand, Lightning was the champion at Marblehead, owned and sailed by Charles Francis Adams, Sec. of the Navy at the time.

On their arrival here in Detroit, Lightning easily sailed away from Bernida and the whole fleet of "R"s. It seemed strange to Russ that Bernida came with 500 pounds of inside ballast. She was very sluggish compared to Lightning. Russ had a pattern made and the inside ballast was melted down and added to the bottom of the keel, making her an absolutely different boat. I was personally involved fabricating the lead shoe on the bottom of the keel. It seems to me that the depth of that shoe was not over 4 inches. Bernida won most every race that year, including the Mackinac.

Russ sailed the boat in 1926 with a medium amount of

Loading The Mast on Bernida—Photo by Jeff Spencer.

success and finally sold her in 1927 to Bobby Bryant. Bernida was not in the 1926 Mackinac, but as you know, Bryant won with her again in 1927.

From the pictures you sent, she looks great. Bernida was always natural finished and a true beauty. As you know, she is double planked, the inside skin of white cedar and the outside of Honduras mahogany. She has white ash frames and keel. The last I'd heard of her, she was in Holland Michigan.

It has been a pleasure for me to recall the story of that wonderful boat and the people involved with her. If there is anything more I can help you with please feel free to write me.

You have a good boat; have many happy sails with her.
Yours Truly,
—Robert K. Roadstrum

In the spring of 1984, Jeff began seriously working on the boat. He launched it in the middle of the summer of 1985 and sailed it in 1986 on Lake Pentwater. He took no one sailing who knew much about the sport and he relied a lot on books about learning how to sail. He also read books about wooden boat building. Someone recommended that he should fiberglass the hull up to the waterline, thinking that this would reduce leaking. He thought it might work, so he did it. When he took the boat out sailing, it leaked so badly that "We didn't think we'd make it back to shore." The hull swelled and cracked the fiberglass in many places. It took the spring of 1986 to remove all of the fiberglass. *Bernida* was launched again in the summer of that year.

In 1986, Jeff, a part time student in engineering at Michigan State University, earned his degree. It was easy to recognize the boat during those years because he had painted it green with the MSU Spartan prominently displayed fore and aft.

Bernida

Jeff Spencer and Friends Crossing Lake Michigan. Photo by Jeff Spencer.

The boat leaked a lot under sail and had the original big brass manual bilge pump which moved a lot of water out. Jeff added an additional auto bilge pump with a float. The boat was dismasted in 1989. He pulled the boat out of the water after the dismasting and ordered some spruce planks from Sitka, Alaska to rebuild the mast in the spring of 1990. After a few years, he got a little bored just sailing around and decided to begin racing against other Pentwater sailors on Lake Michigan during their Saturday races. He got a PHRF rating of 201 for the boat and, after reading more books about racing, actually won many of the twenty five or so races he participated in. With no prior racing experience, he beat many boats with superior equipment and knowledgeable sailors aboard. His sail inventory included a small jib, a 115% genoa and the original mainsail which had to be recut to fix the stretch it incurred.

In 1993, Jeff decided that the boat didn't fit his lifestyle anymore. He was living in Grand Rapids and didn't have the time to spend the hundreds of hours required each spring scraping between the planks, pounding cotton and re-caulking. He used cotton as something to hold the caulk from coming into the boat. The cotton also helped seal the joints as the boat swelled.

He found that the boat was not easy to sell. He was asking $7,500 including a trailer and motor. In 1996, Bob Lucas, a junk dealer in Arcadia, Michigan, came along and saw *Bernida*. Bob was really interested in the boat. He was excited about it and told Jeff he wanted to strip it down and restore it. He didn't want it to hit the "old bone yard." He said he didn't want to pay Jeff's price and asked him to come visit him in Arcadia. Jeff agreed to sell the boat for a shotgun, a 30/30 rifle and a mid 1980's Lincoln Continental. A few weeks later, Jeff really didn't like the car and sold it for $700. He still has the two guns.

"1996 TO 2004"

Bob Lucas owned a business located in Arcadia, Michigan called, "Smoke Stack Junque Shoppe." He bought and sold various things including cars and boats. He also used his large barn-like building as a storage facility for customers who needed storage for large items. When he purchased *Bernida* from Jeff Spencer, he also received a copy of the letter from Bob Roadstrum verifying that this boat was *Bernida*. Lucas originally intended to restore the boat, but after three years of storing it in his barn, he contacted a writer for the Detroit Free Press. Peggy Walsh-Sarnecki traveled to Arcadia and took photos of Lucas and the boat. She wrote an article explaining that the winner of the first Bayview Mackinac Race was now for sale and sitting in a barn in northern Michigan.

Bernida

Bernida

The Comeback Years
1999 to 2012

Toby Murray
"He Found Her"

Bart Huthwaite
"He Bought Her"

Emory Barnwell
"He Restored Her"

Al Declercq
"He Raced Her"

Bernida

Toby Murray
"He Found Her"

Toby Murray was raised on Mackinac Island and it continues to be his summer home. His dad, Latus Murray, owned the Murray Hotel on the Island. The hotel was built by Toby's great-grandfather, an Irish immigrant. Toby's father operated it from 1950 to 1961 when he sold it due to poor health. While working at the hotel every summer, Toby watched all the sailors who arrived at the Island each July as part of the Bayview Yacht Club and Chicago Yacht Club Mackinac Races.

In 1963 Toby graduated from Bowling Green State University with a degree in business and then went on to earn his MBA there in 1964. It was at Bowling Green that he met his future wife, Elaine. Upon graduation, he worked for a bank in Columbus, Ohio for three years and then the family moved to Glendale, Arizona where, in 1968, he earned a degree in International Business at the Thunderbird School of Global Management.

After his time at Thunderbird, Toby went to work for JP Morgan in New York. Most of his work was with U.S. multinational companies, advising and assisting them financially with their overseas operations. In January of 1975 while Toby was hosting a lunch with three Morgan clients and two fellow bankers at a famous New York restaurant, Fraunces Tavern, the Puerto Rican National Liberation Movement (FALN) placed a bomb behind a metal fire exit door right next to where Toby and his friends were seated. When it exploded, the door turned into shrapnel and sprayed the occupants in the restaurant. Three men were killed at his table and Toby suffered multiple injuries leaving him with a hearing loss and the loss of sight in one eye. After months spent recovering, he returned to work and attempted to bring to his job the same energy and enthusiasm he always had, but he recognized his heart was not in it and he decided he wanted to spend more time closer to his family.

Since he had such fond memories of working with his father at the Murray Hotel, he and Elaine looked for an inn to buy in Vermont and in January of 1978 purchased the Three Mountain Inn. Close to three skiing mountains, it was located in Jamaica, Vermont. The Inn initially had just seven guest rooms but was expanded over time to a total of seventeen rooms in three buildings. The original home was built in 1795. Elaine did all the cooking. In 1999 the Murray's sold their Inn after 21 years of serving thousands of guests and bought their current home on 250 acres up in the woods in the nearby town of West Townshend, VT.

On August 24, 1999 the saga of *Bernida* took a great leap forward while Toby was reading the *Detroit Free Press* and fell upon an article written by Peggy Walsh-Sarnecki, which appeared, of all places, in the Body and Mind section of the paper.

The article was entitled, "The Owner of a Historic Boat Is Ready to Turn Over the Helm." It went on to state that the boat for sale was the 1925 original Bayview Mackinac Race winner, *Bernida*. It also included a photo of the owner, Bob Lucas of Arcadia, Michigan with the boat itself in his warehouse behind him. Having grown up on Mackinac Island, Toby knew the history of the race and was immediately excited by the news that *Bernida* had been located.

Toby immediately called Bob Lucas, who told him that he had some old letters that proved the authenticity of his claim

Bernida

*Original Detroit Free Press Article Announcing Bernida For Sale.
Photo by Toby Murray.*

that this boat was *Bernida*. In the summer of 2000, Toby traveled to Arcadia to see the boat for himself. During that visit, he made copies of two letters written by Bob Roadstrum, a Bayview Yacht Club member and the last living member of the fleet that raced in 1925. His letters contained many details and made a very strong case that this was *Bernida*. The boat was being offered for sale by one of Bob Lucas's companies, Boiler Room Trading. Lucas was asking $10,000 for *Bernida* and Toby, not having the funds himself to purchase the boat, decided to keep his discovery a secret until he could find a donor. Toby was afraid someone from the Bayview Yacht Club would find the boat and buy it. He felt strongly that *Bernida* could be used to promote a youth sailing program on Mackinac Island. Sometime after seeing the boat, Toby hired Jay Altmaier, a wooden boat craftsman from the Les Cheneaux Islands, to survey the boat and see if the boat could be salvaged. Altmaier came back with his answer on November 26, 2001. In his letter, he listed the considerable number of repairs needed and summarized his report with the familiar words, "All it takes is money."

The following are a series of letters written between Toby and Bob Roadstrum which began with a letter from Toby dated April 14, 2002.

Dear Robert,

…A few summers ago I saw an ad for a sailboat for sale, which was advertised as the Bernida, the boat that won the first Port Huron to Mackinac Race. … I was on Mackinac Island at the time. My family is from Mackinac—actually my great grandfather, Dominick, came over from Ireland in the 1860's and decided to settle there…. Growing up, I spent every summer there and many summers I worked with my dad at the Murray Hotel in the center of town right at the head of the Arnold dock. The possibility that this boat might be the winner of the first race was very exciting.

…I finally did get a chance to view the boat. It was then that he (Bob Lucas) gave me copies of your letters written to a previous owner along with some other details on the boat. Obviously, the boat I saw was not in good shape and needed lots of work. However, I wanted to pursue the matter further and based on your information, I was actually able to track down copies of the architectural drawings from the Historical Nautical Museum at MIT. As a next step I am going to try and track the builders if they still exist. I also had a boat renovator from Les Cheneaux look the boat over to try and come up with a rough idea as to what it might cost to renovate the Bernida.

Bernida

…My feelings are strong that such a wonderful part of yachting history should not end up in some warehouse with green paint on it. At the moment, I am living a pipedream: I would like to organize a small foundation and go out and look for some grants to get the work done and then to set up a program on the Island that would make sailing accessible to the Island youth. It's a strange thing—they see two races each year from Chicago and Port Huron, and they see beautiful sailboats all summer, but there is no opportunity whatsoever for them to participate in the activity that should be a natural extension of their lives. Many of them are from poor backgrounds and it is my feeling this would be an incredible opportunity for them to build their own self esteem. It will take some work to get it all organized, but I want to make the attempt. It would be fantastic to both save a beautiful sailboat with its wonderful history and at the same time have the kids up there involved in the process.

Anyway, I'd like to hear from you and meet you if possible when I come out late in the month of May. I know in 1984, when you wrote those letters, it was quite a while ago, so I hope this finds you in good health….
—Toby Murray

Dear Toby Murray,
In response to your inquiry as to the possibility of rebuilding the Bernida, I don't want to break your heart, but the answer is no! When the young man who acquired her rebuilt her and covered the hull with fiberglass that was the beginning of the end for that wonderful yacht.
—Robert K. Roadstrum

May 5, 2002

…Robert, you may be absolutely correct about the hopelessness of putting the Bernida back together, but I haven't given up yet. When I'm on the Island, I am going to take the plans over to the wooden boat restorer I have talked to and have him explain exactly what is involved and the costs.
—Toby Murray

Toby,
I'm sorry if my answer was abrupt. But in today's market, rebuilding Bernida would run over $50,000. But your idea has a great deal of merit. Getting an owner to contribute the plans of his winning boat displayed on a half model made with a large backboard showing the class of his boat also when and what she won in the race would be great. Also the crew list.
—Robert K. Roadstrum

Bernida at Smoke Stack Junque Shoppe in Arcadia, Michigan.
Photo by Toby Murray.

Bernida

    One year after the exchange of letters with Bob Roadstrum, Toby called a friend on the Island asking, "Who do we have on Mackinac who is a doer?" Without missing a beat, the friend responded, "Bart Huthwaite", who is a longtime Island resident and member of the Mackinac Island Yacht Club. Toby then wrote a long letter to Bart describing the entire history of *Bernida*, its current condition and his vision of having *Bernida* serve as motivation for a youth sailing program. Toby did not hear back from Bart, but the following summer while Toby was working at the Mackinac Island State Dock, Bart came up to him and said, "Toby, we have to talk." Toby showed him all the historical provenance as well as a copy of the boat's original architectural drawings he had collected and Bart said, "Let's go look at it."

    They drove to Arcadia and tried to negotiate the price with Bob Lucas. (Toby had prepared three typed Purchase Contracts: one for $5,000, one for $7500, and one for $10,000, depending on how the negotiations might go.) Lucas, however, jumped up screaming, "No! no! no!" Bart said, "Ok, ok, we'll pay you the $10,000. I'll write a check now and I'll send a bank check tomorrow."

    They had the boat hauled across the Mackinac Bridge to St. Ignace where it was stored at the Arnold Ferry Line's Mill Slip. It was shipped on the same cradle Jeff Spencer included in his sale to Bob Lucas. Now that they owned it, they needed to know how much it would cost to have the boat restored so she could be sailed again. Bart wanted the best professional wood restorer he could find. He called Dave Irish, the owner of the Irish Boat Shop in Harbor Springs, MI. His restorer made a list of all necessary repairs and arrived at a cost of $175,000 to get the boat back to its original condition. Bart, "the Mackinac doer",

Bernida

was not to be deterred by the quote.

It became obvious they would have to form a 501(C)3 foundation to raise the money, and thus the new owner of *Bernida* became "The Mackinac Island Yacht Club Great Turtle Foundation". At its first meeting, the following were in attendance: Bart Huthwaite, Toby Murray, David Rowe, Jack Keck and Dick Cregar. The group established three goals for the *Bernida* project: to provide an artifact for restoration to preserve a wonderful piece of the Straits maritime history, to educate Mackinac youth in the history of the Great Lakes, and to encourage and teach the sport of sailing to the Island's youth. They also considered three levels of restoration: a "show" boat, a "go" boat, or a "Hessel" boat (lots of "show", but not much "go"). At that meeting, three new board members were proposed; Jim Rogers, Jack Kote and Ted Everingham, the then Commodore of Bayview Yacht Club.

While actively trying to line up donors, Toby had a gnawing thought: What if this is not *Bernida*? Could this be just another old wooden R Boat with the same dimensions? Recalling Bob Roadstrum's story that Russ Pouliot had added six inches of lead to the original keel, Toby immediately went over to St. Ignace and measured *Bernida*'s keel comparing her keel dimensions to George Owen's original design prints. Sure enough the keel was 6" longer and when he looked very closely, he spotted a miniscule line running down the length of the shoe where it joined the original keel. Obviously very relieved, they continued their efforts at fund raising.

To help with their efforts, the two decided to bring *Bernida* from St. Ignace to Mackinac Island and display the boat at the entrance to the Mission Point Resort, which was the headquarters for the Bayview Mackinac Race. They wanted all

Bernida

the hundreds of sailors coming for the annual party and awards ceremony to see the boat and, hopefully, contribute to the restoration project. They found, however, that few of the sailors had any interest. Very discouraged, they shipped *Bernida* back to St. Ignace where she remained in her cradle for two more years.

BART HUTHWAITE
"He Bought Her"

Bart Huthwaite is a vital contributor to the story of *Bernida* because he is the person who rescued *Bernida* from obscurity in an old barn in northern Michigan. He paid the full asking price of $10,000 from his own funds so that the boat could race again in a Mackinac Race. He then contributed more than $20,000 to begin restoration of the boat and to fund a campaign to raise the money to complete the project.

Bart is known on Mackinac Island for his leadership in keeping the *Bernida* dream alive through the four years it took to find a person skilled and dedicated to restoring the boat. Hundreds of people, both on the Island and off, were part of this saga.

Mackinac Island sailing is his passion. Island locals do not have a long history of sailing. A major reason was the lack of dockage. Huthwaite formed the Mackinac Island Harbor Club to create moorings for Island residents. He held a Lightning Class regatta that drew more than 25 boats from across the Midwest to build interest in sailing. Huthwaite donated a 24 foot sailboat called *Island Girl* to teach high school students to sail. He wrote a weekly column in the Town Crier, the local paper, entitled "Dock Lines". He funded a foundation to benefit boating programs on the Island.

Bart comes from a successful business background and is the founder of the Huthwaite Innovation Institute, a global company that educates engineers on how to design products that cost less, get to market faster, and with better quality. After founding his own machine tool company in Troy, Michigan, he helped Ford Motor Company by building an automated assembly line. He introduced an exciting concept to the people at Ford; design products with their assembly and maintenance needs in mind. Ford was so pleased, the company asked him to teach Ford how to design their own assembly lines with his concepts. Bart realized that there was a huge market for automated assembly line design consultants. So, he sold his machine tool company to a partner and began a very lucrative career as a consultant with major clients including Microsoft, General Dynamics and General Motors.

His wife, Nina Huthwaite, had created a thriving business selling brass nautical replicas of everything from ship's wheels to sailing lanterns at boat shows. Harry Ryba, the famous

L to R: Bob Lucas, Toby Murray & Bart Huthwaite Concluding the Purchase. Photo by Toby Murray.

Mackinac fudge maker, suggested at a boat show that she take her business to Mackinac Island during the summer. The result was the "Nina's Nautical Brass" shop on Main Street and a new summer home on the Island. Their family moved to Mackinac Island in the late 80's where Bart eventually became Commodore of the Mackinac Island Yacht Club.

Bart and Toby had many objectives to accomplish. First and foremost, they wanted to see *Bernida* race in the annual Bayview Mackinac Race again. They also hoped to use her to revitalize interest in family sailing. Another objective was to preserve the history of *Bernida* and of Great Lakes sailing. The boat could also serve as a great training boat for Island kids learning to sail. They wanted to stimulate interest in Mackinac Island as a visitor maritime destination. Finally, they hoped that *Bernida* would become the flagship of a summer sailing program.

The fundraising efforts began in earnest in the summer of 2005. They had hats and shirts which were sold to raise money. They conducted island-wide raffles and accepted small donations. They got the local press involved to promote the fundraising effort. They tried to persuade the members at Bayview to help out. Some people were interested, but nothing came of it.

In August of 2005, Bart asked Jeff Steiner if he would write a song about *Bernida*. Jeff wrote the song and music in one night and performed "Sail on for me *Bernida*" at a dinner at the Mackinac Island Yacht Club on August 11. He did an outstanding job in such short order. The song has beautiful words and music and many verses:

Sail On For Me My Bernida—Copyright 2013 by Jeff Steiner

There once was a sloop full of spirit and grace
  her owner he called her Bernida
She sailed on the lakes at a furious pace
  so quick she won the inaugural race

Chorus
Sail on sail on, sail on for me my Bernida
Sail on sail on, sail on for me my Bernida

Born from a legend, George Owen his name,
She first hailed from Boston of MIT fame
This ship was the pride of the east coast fleet,
An opponent most others would not want to meet.

Chorus
The time it had come to make her debut,
in Michigan no less new owner and crew
In `25 She hailed from Bayview I guess,
with skipper Russ Pouliot sporting his best

Chorus
On a damp, murky day she was readied to race
with her crew and good captain starting to pace
Riding a swell she crashed through the rain
with lightning and thunder a broad reach she strained

Chorus
Her crew remained steady, focused and true
for the sweet sight of Mackinac would soon be in view
12 boats began, only four boats remained
and Bernida was receiving the fortune and fame.

Bernida

Last Chorus
First race, first place – sail on your way my Bernida
First race, first place – sail on your way my Bernida
Sail on sail on, sail on for me my Bernida
Sail on sail on, sail on for me my Bernida

In addition to the struggle to raise money, they had great difficulty finding someone who had the woodworking skills to actually bring *Bernida* back. They found a woodworker in St. Ignace who wanted to start restoring the boat. He began working on the hull, but it did not work out. The sailing seasons of 2006 and 2007 went by without much progress while the boat remained covered at the Arnold yard in St. Ignace.

Near the end of 2007, Bart received a phone call from Becky Barnwell, the owner of the Iroquois Hotel on the island. She told him that her son, Emory, would be returning soon from a wooden boat restoration school he had been attending in England. She felt, perhaps, he could get involved in the *Bernida* project. Before Emory left for England, he had worked as a carpenter on the restoration of a store on the Island and used the scrap wood to build a sailboat which he sailed himself. What a break! Not only did Emory have the credentials to restore *Bernida*, but he was an Island resident who would be available year round to move the project forward.

Emory returned from England and was back on the Island in the summer of 2008. He met Bart at a very well known local restaurant called The Pink Pony. When Bart shook hands with him, he realized he had the hands of a carpenter. The agreement was that Emory would take title to the boat in return for restoring it. Bart emphasized to Emory that he wanted to see the boat restored so that she could race once again in the

Bart Huthwaite, Commodore Mackinac Island Yacht Club.
Photo by Bart Huthwaite.

Bayview Mackinac Race. Finally, the craftsman was found and the long awaited restoration of *Bernida* was going to become a reality.

ROMAN "EMORY" BARNWELL
"He Restored Her"

Roman Emory Barnwell (Emory) was a key player in the *Bernida* saga. He always had an interest in carpentry and enjoyed woodworking and art classes in school. He built paddles for the kayaks and canoes he took out on Michigan's lakes. He attended the University of Montana and graduated in 2005 with a degree in Recreation Management from its College of Forestry and Conservation.

The following fall he enrolled in the International Boat Building Training College located in Lowestoft, England. Its curriculum emphasized a hands-on environment. Learning-

Bernida

by-doing suited Emory just fine. Students needed to be self motivated because they weren't getting graded on tests, only results. The student to instructor ratio was 5 to 1 or 7 to 1. He started in the joinery shop in order to learn the basics and then moved into the boat building course. He had to complete a list of accomplishments and then move on from one project to the next. He graduated at the top of his class because he pushed himself hard while reading and learning all he could about the essentials of boat design. The school's website features a great quote from Emory on its homepage: "In my work, there is not a minute that passes that is not enjoyed to the fullest." Roman Barnwell, Class of 2007.

He returned to his home on Mackinac Island in 2007. Shortly afterwards, he built a dinghy sailboat which was prominently displayed in the Crooked Tree Art Center in downtown Petoskey, Michigan. His grandma, mom and brothers lived on Mackinac Island in the summer. Emory sent resumes around to boat building companies hoping to utilize his training in England. He had some interviews, but the economy was

Emory Barnwell Aboard Bernida. Photo by Andre Dupre.

weakening and customers were backing out of big boat building jobs which would require more workers. The states of Maine and Washington had certain harbors where wooden boats were numerous, but they weren't hiring either. So, he got jobs as a carpenter on the Island.

In 2008, he was at the Mills Slip in St. Ignace one day and saw an old wooden sailboat sitting on its cradle outside. He didn't know anything about the fund raising efforts underway to restore the boat. It looked to him like it was just sitting over there abandoned. He met with Bart Huthwaite and agreed to restore *Bernida* if he was given the boat's title. Bart agreed and Emory became *Bernida*'s newest owner. Because the Mill Slip in St. Ignace is the property of Arnold Line, Emory went to talk to Bob Brown, its manager. As fate will have it, Bob has always been a lifelong wooden boat person. He agreed to provide Emory with space on its Coal Dock on Mackinac Island where he could work on the boat. Bob agreed to move the boat back and forth between St. Ignace and the Island whenever necessary. He also provided hoists, tools, and utilities.

Emory got the boat delivered to the Coal Dock in the fall of 2008. He built a shelter so that he could house the boat and work on it year round. He had it sitting on a trailer with jack stands. He took the trailer's wheels off and removed the lead keel. The restoration began by replacing wood from the keel upward. All floor timbers had to go. About 95% of the frame was replaced. He kept 80% of the planking and built a whole new deck. Emory said the ballast keel was original as is 60% of the wooden keel. He was very determined to restore *Bernida* to its original design.

His new deck structure and spar design were from the original drawings housed at the museum at MIT. He was very

Bernida During Restoration Process (Top: Early Stage; Bottom: Later Stage). Photo by Emory Barnwell.

surprised and grateful that the designs were available. Toby Murray, who originally discovered the boat in 1999, also provided him the MIT drawings. It was quite obvious to Emory that interim owners had made many changes over the years. The original fastenings and meticulous workmanship done in 1921 were proof the *Bernida* was built by the top craftsmen of the time.

He thought the mast, rigging and boom were good, but when they took them out of the shed, he realized the mast was rotten from the inside out. It wasn't the original mast and he decided to build a whole new rig according to the details shown in the original drawings. A lot of friends in the off season pitched in to help. It had become quite a topic of discussion, particularly among the few winter residents who remained on the Island.

Emory didn't have much money. The whole project was very stressful for him. As he kept peeling back sections of the boat, he tried to keep what he could. When he had to purchase new lumber, he used the same wood that was originally used. The ribs were made of white oak. He used copper rivets. The planking was Honduran mahogany.

The deck beams were white oak. The original deck was canvas covered. He restored it with marine plywood which gave the deck greater dimensional stability and made it stronger. He finished it with painted canvas over the top using the same finish as was on the original deck. Emory wanted to take the boat sailing and he thought the additional strengthening was worth doing. He paid for all the materials out of his own pocket. The complete restoration took all of his savings ($15,000) and two years of his life working full time.

During the winter of 2010, Bart Huthwaite contacted Al Declercq of Doyle Sails Detroit in hopes that he could help

Bernida

Emory with sails for *Bernida*. In March of 2010, Al Declercq, his wife Sara and son Matthew flew up to see the finished boat. They measured it for sails and gave Emory a new mainsail and jib.

Equipped with a new mast that he made and new sails, the restored *Bernida* was launched in the summer of 2010. He took it out sailing four or five times that summer. Al's donated new sails were a big help to Emory because he had no money left for sails. He also didn't have money for hardware, so he built wooden blocks and sailed it around the harbor. It was fun.

That August, Emory decided to sail *Bernida* to the Les Cheneaux Islands' Antique Wooden Boat Show held each year in Hessel, Michigan in the Upper Peninsula. One mile out of Mackinac Island's harbor, however, he broke a shroud on the portside and had to turn back. At the end of August, he pulled

Bernida Finished Interior—Photo by Jeffrey Dupre.

the boat and stored the new mast inside. Emory was becoming desperate to recoup his money. He tried to generate interest at yacht clubs with no success. As the summer of 2011 came along, he didn't put the boat in the water. He couldn't afford to store it or insure it. Having exhausted all options, Emory decided to put *Bernida* up for bid on eBay.

During the entire restoration process, Al Declercq had been following the plight of *Bernida*. Shortly after it was posted on eBay, Al received a call telling him *Bernida* was listed on eBay. He called Emory and told him that if he would take it off eBay, he would pay the $15,000 asking price and would race *Bernida* in the 2012 Bayview Mackinac Race. Emory reviewed with Al the items that would require additional work and Al didn't believe that any of the problems would be difficult to correct.

Al Declercq and Emory Barnwell Confirming the Mast Measurements. Photo by Sara Declercq.

Bernida

Al said he wanted to take the rigging to the next level so it would be strong enough for the race. Al asked Emory to tighten bolts and fix up the paint job. Emory learned, as did so many owners before him, that it is tough to get someone interested in buying a 90 year old wooden boat.

Bernida with Restoration Completed on Mackinac Island.
Photo by Andre Dupre

Looking back on the experience, Emory was happy to sell it for enough money to at least cover his costs. He spent two years, seven days per week for the last eighteen months of the project working on *Bernida*. He also had a lot of help from other people on the Island and is very grateful for their assistance and encouragement.

Bernida

AL DECLERCQ
"He Raced Her"

PREPARATION FOR 2012 MACKINAC RACE

Note: All text printed in Italics hereafter is Al Declercq's first person narrative.

Al Declercq has a BBA from Eastern Michigan University and an MBA from the University of Detroit. After a couple of years with Chrysler Corporation, he went into the sail making business when he started North Sails Detroit in September of 1979, followed by UK Sailmakers Detroit in 1989, and his present business, Doyle Sails Detroit founded in 2006 and located in Clinton Township, Michigan.

In addition to making sails, Al has been a very avid and highly successful competitive sailor logging more than 50,000 miles of offshore racing experience. He sailed in his first Mackinac Race in 1966 on his dad's boat, *Flying Buffalo* when he was twelve years old. He only missed one race since then when he sailed in the TransPac Race in 2005 with Fred Detwiler aboard his TP52, *Trader*. At the writing of this book in 2013, he has completed 36 Chicago Mackinac Races and 45 Port Huron Mackinac races. He has a total of 24 first place Mackinac finishes.

He has also been very successful in international ocean races resulting in more than 21 first place finishes. These races have included six Newport to Bermuda races, five Marblehead to Halifax races, four Fort Lauderdale to Montego Bay races, four Newport to Cabo San Lucas races, one Transpac race, five Trans Superior races, five Trans Erie races, sixteen Key West races and numerous NOOD and One Design regattas.

Bernida

I think it is fair to say that although Al encountered numerous naysayers about his dream of racing *Bernida* in the 2012 Bell's Beer Bayview Mackinac Race, his confidence in a successful outcome was bolstered by many years of "being out there."

The following are Al's personal recollections of his *Bernida* adventure accompanied by the recollections of those involved in preparing and racing her:

> It all started when Ted Everingham approached me at the Mackinac awards party in the summer of 2006 and introduced me to Bart Huthwaite. Bart was heading up a group, along with Roman Barnwell, that was restoring *Bernida*. Roman did a beautiful job restoring *Bernida*. I suspect the boat looks better today than when she won the first Mackinac race.

Ted Everingham was Commodore of Bayview Yacht Club in 2003. He has been a very active member of the club for many years and is well known throughout the Grosse Pointes for his cable television show, "Great Lakes Log," writings in Grosse Pointe Magazine and many other community related activities.

He is the person who made Al Declercq aware of Bart Huthwaite and his fund raising efforts to restore *Bernida* to racing form. Ted learned about Bart when reading an article that appeared in the Mackinac Island Town Crier. Subsequently, Ted spoke with Bart and discussed how difficult it was to raise money for such an undertaking. Ted showed *Bernida* to Al when they were both on Mackinac Island after a race.

Ted, who has sailed many Bayview Mackinac races himself, was very excited to think of *Bernida* sailing the same race course that she sailed in 1925. He remembers Al saying to him, "If the wind is right, we can win this thing." As Ted remembers, "I was not on the boat, but I was kind of along in spirit." He saw the beginning of the race and knew they had a good start. He also thought *Bernida*'s attempt was made all the more special because the crew was composed of three lifelong friends and their sons.

Sara Declercq is the wife of Al Declercq and an accomplished sailor herself. Her childhood years were spent sailing with her family all over the Great Lakes in the family's Cal 40. Sara has a degree in Packaging from Michigan State University. Upon graduation, she went to work for the Michigan Department of Transportation. After a year, her parents encouraged her to pursue her interests in sailing. They told her that life was too short to not follow your dreams. She took her engineering skills to North Sails where she was hired to design and implement a computer network system. She went to work for the Detroit loft owner at the time, Al Declercq. After a year and a half, they began dating and as Sara puts it, "The rest is history."

Eventually, Al and Sara decided to start their own sail loft which became UK Sailmakers and ultimately, Doyle Sails Detroit. In order to provide cash flow to enable them to build the new business, Sara went to work for Crain's Detroit, a business publisher, for seven years. She also remained actively involved with their sail loft. Presently, she and Al run the Doyle loft together.

The Declercqs have two children, Allison, a junior at the University of California, Berkeley and Matthew, a senior at Grosse Pointe South High School. As related elsewhere in this book, Matthew played a major role in the *Bernida* story. Allison had already arranged to study in Europe in the summer of 2012 and unfortunately missed most of the *Bernida* attempt to conquer the Bayview Mackinac race once again.

Being long time members of the Bayview Yacht Club, both Al and Sara were familiar with the history of the Mackinac Race and the first winner, *Bernida*. When Al was introduced by Ted Everingham to Bart Huthwaite in 2006, he learned that a group on Mackinac Island had located *Bernida* and wanted to restore it and race it again. Four years later, Al, Sara and their son Matthew flew up to Mackinac Island in March of 2010 to see the boat and meet Emory Barnwell, the young boat builder and its owner at the time.

They measured the boat for sails and returned home and built a new mainsail and jib so that Emory could sail the boat once completed. These sails were donated to Emory because the Declercqs thought it was a nice thing to do. Later, in the summer of 2010, Al and Sara saw Emory sailing *Bernida* off Mackinac Island. The sight of *Bernida* ghosting along in five knots of breeze, just outside the Mackinac Island break wall, made Sara and Al proud that they had donated the sails.

In the summer of 2011, Al was talking seriously about wanting to buy *Bernida* and sail her in the 2012 Mackinac race. By that time, Emory had decided to put the boat up for auction on eBay. He was asking $15,000.

This did not set well with me. I believed the boat should stay in the area and I was concerned that someone from one of the active fleets in Seattle, Cleveland, or Toronto would purchase the boat. So after a few beers at Dead Man's Curve (the far corner of the Bayview Yacht Club bar), I gave Emory a call and told him I would buy the boat if he pulled it off eBay. We agreed to a price, as Jerome handed me my next beer, and the quest to win a third Mackinac Race for Bernida began.

Prior to buying the boat from Emory, Al met with the Board of Bayview Yacht Club in 2011 to see if the club would allow him to enter *Bernida* in the upcoming 2012 Bayview Mackinac Race. He stated he would not buy the boat if he couldn't race her. It would obviously require some variances from the standard racing rules in order for *Bernida* to be allowed to compete. The Board agreed, provided that Al would work out the details with the chairman of the 2012 race, Greg Thomas.

Greg Thomas has been a member of Bayview Yacht Club since 1988. He also served as race chairman for the 2002 race and was Commodore in 2005. He initially heard that *Bernida* had been found and was being restored on Mackinac Island from Bart Huthwaite in an email. When on the island after a race, Greg saw *Bernida* at the entrance to Mission Point Resort. He was shocked to see how small and narrow the boat was and what a small amount of freeboard she had.

In the fall of 2011, Al Declercq told Greg that he was considering the purchase of *Bernida* for the purpose of racing her in the upcoming 2012 race. Greg decided to specifically name *Bernida* in the Notice of Race (NOR) and said she would race under amended rules based upon the discretion of the race committee. These rules, after meeting with Al, dealt with safety equipment and procedures which would be employed under certain weather conditions. Below is the posting in the 2012 Notice of Race:

> **2012 NOTICE OF RACE Section 2-d**
>
> For monohulls, the Mackinac Safety Regulations 2012 – Monohulls ("MSR"). The winner of the inaugural Mackinac Race in 1925, *Bernida*, is expected to apply to sail in the race. Due to the historic nature of its participation and constraints that may make it impossible to comply in all respects with the MSR, the Race Committee reserves the right to modify and/or supplement the MSR as it relates to *Bernida*, alone.

Bernida was being prepared for the race at Bayview all through the winter and the spring of 2012 and Greg watched the effort to make her race ready. He used to joke with Al and

Bernida

Sara Declercq, "You guys will end up swimming ashore." He thought, as did many others, that if they had the wrong wind conditions, *Bernida* would not finish the race.

There were a few structural issues that needed to be addressed, and I figured who better than Emory Barnwell to fix the problems before we picked Bernida up in St.Ignace in the fall of 2011.

Roman through bolted a few planks that had been secured by wood screws and spruced up the top sides and bright work. The boat was delivered to Bayview Yacht Club shortly before Christmas by Gary Snider.

In order to complete the preparation of *Bernida* for the grueling Mackinac Race ahead, Al employed the services of three very highly skilled craftsmen; Todd Jones, Andy Groh and Dean Kuhn.

In December of 2011, he approached Todd Jones who is the owner of Thomas Hardware on Mack Avenue in Grosse Pointe Farms, MI. Thomas Hardware has been supplying the sailing community the world over since 1919. Its slogan is, "Everything for sailboats."

Andy Groh is a mechanical engineer who previously worked

Bernida Arriving at Bayview Yacht Club.
Photo by Kevin Schrage.

for Offshore Spars on the construction of large carbon fiber masts. He also has designed many rigging systems. Like almost everyone else mentioned in this book, Andy is a very experienced sailor who has been racing since age ten.

They began with the basic sail plan Al wanted, which would include a mast head code zero, a high roach main, spinnakers and other headsails. The newly designed rig would have to provide sufficient head stay tension and hold up to any weather conditions they would encounter. They began talking globally. Al thought the existing rigging was well intentioned but not right for the racing conditions it could encounter. He wanted to be sure the boat would survive the rigors of the Mackinac Race and continue to be viable after the race and into the future.

Andy was coming out of a background designing with carbon fiber, thus making a big transition to working with wood. He took out old books that dealt with the standards of wooden mast design. There was a higher probability of failures when loading up a hollow wooden mast. Wood has imperfections, such as knots, that have to be anticipated when making rigging decisions.

Working with Todd Jones, Andy came up with spreader attachments and a masthead that would be able to hoist the sails. He suggested hardware and various means of attachment to the rigging. The biggest concern was the possible fatigue in the metal attachments used to attach the fittings to the hollow wooden mast. He also suggested how the boom vang should attach.

Looking back with hindsight, Andy said, "I knew the rig would hold up, but I didn't know how the boat would hold up. The boat was definitely the weak point. The rigging was a mathematical certainty, but I didn't know about the hull and deck." He thought it was a great idea to enter *Bernida* in the race and that it would be a great challenge for the crew. He also liked the idea of resurrecting history. Andy said he would like to see more sailors take on this type of challenge in the future.

Of course, Todd knew the story of *Bernida*'s great victory in the inaugural 1925 Mackinac race. When he saw it for the first time at Bayview Yacht Club, he was surprised to see how small it was. He thought the guys were brave to enter it in the annual Mackinac Race.

Al Declercq had called Todd and told him that he needed the boat's mast re-rigged and a place to store the rig indoors for the winter. He wanted to make it stronger and able to carry bigger sails. Todd met with Andy Groh, who calculated the loads the rig would have to handle. It was a new mast, but needed stronger rigging. Todd knew he had to make it happen on a wooden spar. Todd graciously stored the rig at Thomas Hardware for the winter.

He spent forty hours reconfiguring the whole mast. It needed a new masthead that would fly spinnakers for the first time. He designed a masthead cap which would have to support running backstays and blocks for spinnakers halyards. One of the decisions was to add an additional set of spreaders to support the added load from the higher tech sails.

They used all the technology necessary to get the boat ready to race and stay together over such a long distance.

Thomas Hardware also supplied a double diaphragm bilge pump and an electric pump so that *Bernida* could handle the situation if they encountered heavy weather. Todd felt it was a great experience putting the boat together and he was glad to be a part of it.

Our first concern was with the rig. It was a single spreader

Mast Stepped at Bayview Yacht Club.
Photo by Sara Declercq.

rig and the panel length between the supporting shrouds was too long to provide adequate support. Andy Groh re-designed the rig and added a second set of spreaders. The two spreader configuration, and modern top mast and running backstay system, should ensure we can make it to the finish line without someone yelling "TIMBER!" We moved the head stay up two feet to optimize the "I" dimension to the R Boat rule, and modified the masthead unit to accept masthead spinnakers. This seemed like the easiest way to get the sail area up to the limit allowed by the rule. The other option was to increase the "J" dimension, and although the boat would have been a little faster with a longer "J", it would have required much more work and money, and we wanted to sail the boat in a similar upwind configuration as in the 1925 Mackinac race. The mast redesign was completed March 1, 2012. On March 9, we finalized the new deck hardware layout and ordered parts after consulting with Todd Jones .

On April 6, three of Al's family members began the work of reinforcing all high load areas where new winches, track, and pad eyes were to be installed. The three people were David LaMere (Sara's brother), Bob LaMere (Sara's dad) and the Declercqs' son Matthew. The boat was plenty strong enough to go for a day sail, but not strong enough to sail under racing loads.

Sara had some concerns and apprehension about the whole project. Her dad told her about all the wood they were installing on the boat to give it the strength required to survive Lake Huron. As it added strength, it was also adding weight to a boat that was designed with very little freeboard. She knew the size of the guys sailing and the amount of gear that they would have to take on the race. Adding weight was a concern. Her dad came home often and said I think Al might be loading the boat with too many sails and forces that it was never designed for. During the months leading up to the race, Sara made numerous trips to the boat to bring Matthew something to eat because he was going straight from school to the boat and working till dark. She also helped them with whatever they needed. As she began to see the improvements Matthew and her dad were making to *Bernida*, her earlier concerns were quelled. She also trusted Al and his judgment. She knew he would take all the necessary precautions to make the crew as safe as possible, and she was excited to be a part of the adventure.

Sara Declercq's brother, David LaMere, was the first person Al asked to work on the boat. He is a graduate of the Great Lakes Maritime Academy in Traverse City, Michigan. He has many years of sailboat racing and maintenance experience. David has logged thousands of miles racing offshore with Al. He is now a measurer of racing sailboats. His job is to take a boat's measurements and use them to calculate the rating for each boat. There are three times reported on each boat as it crosses the finish line. These are: the time it finished, the actual elapsed time from the start to the finish and the corrected time which is a computation of the actual time and a rating factor. Race finishers are compared on their corrected time. This allows faster and slower boats to compete against each other.

When Sara first told David that they bought *Bernida* and would enter her in the 2012 Bayview Mackinac Race, it sounded a little crazy to him. David has raced with Al in several offshore races including the 2005 TransPac with Fred Detwiler. He also has raced with Matthew in addition to logging hundreds of delivery miles with him. David thought the idea of racing *Bernida* promised to be a great adventure. He felt a little better

Bernida

about it knowing they would sail the shore course. In the spring of 2012, he helped Al redesign the deck layout on *Bernida* in order to make it a little more race friendly and to strengthen several areas. He also installed hardware for the jib and main sails. Despite the improvements being made to the boat, David felt that it would be a wet ride because it was so small and would carry a six man crew. He spent about two weeks working on the boat.

   At this writing, Al and Sara's son, Matthew Declercq, is 17 years old. His passion for sailing started at a young age. His first sail was with his grandfather on the family's Cal 40 when he was just two months old. He went on several delivery trips with his Uncle David and his grandpa. Sara was often with them too. He learned how to sail at the Bayview Yacht Club junior sailing program and sailing with Al. He was sailing competitively at age 7 and later became a sailing coach at the club. He sailed in his first Bayview Mackinac Race in 2007 on a North American 40. This was a father and son crew organized by Ken Flaska and served as a model for *Bernida*. He has now completed five Bayview Mackinac races and two Chicago to Mackinac races. Although leading a busy life as a junior at Grosse Pointe South High School, Matthew played a vital role in preparing *Bernida* to race again.

   He first saw *Bernida* in the spring of 2010 when he flew up to Mackinac Island with his mom and dad a year before Al bought the boat. About one year later, after his dad bought the boat, he drove down to Bayview to see it again. It was a boat, a mast and boom and no hardware. It became apparent to Matthew that it needed a lot of work. Matthew, with the help of his grandpa, Bob LaMere, began adding the necessary hardware and electronics *Bernida* would need to become competitive.

Bernida

They worked on the boat throughout the spring of 2012 right up until, and including, the day of the race. Every day after school, Matthew would drive to the boat and work until dark. Once school finished in early June, he started coaching junior sailing and went right to work on *Bernida* after coaching all day. He spent most of his weekends with *Bernida* as well. This was a giant commitment for a seventeen year old and Matthew demonstrated devotion that impressed everyone involved with the *Bernida* project.

 One day stands out in Sara's mind. The daily work on *Bernida* was tiring for Matthew. On the morning of his physics final exam, she woke him up before she left for work. He, however, fell back to sleep and would be late for his exam. He called Sara to tell her what had happened. After talking with the physics teacher, he was allowed to start the exam 15 minutes late. All turned out well as he set the curve for his class and the entire physics department with a score of 106.

 Matthew said that his grandpa, who built his own house, had a lot of knowledge he didn't have. Papa came down to the boat at 9AM on weekends and worked until dark. He was also there every day after school. Matthew liked having a second person to brainstorm solutions to the many problems they faced. He always liked engineering and took as many woodshop classes as his high school would allow.

 There was always a long list of repairs and improvements that had to be made. The boat was damaged in three preliminary races and several new items were always added to the list. After the first race, the deck had to be strengthened with pressure treated 2 X 6 and 2 X 8 planks. All additional wood used to strengthen the platforms for the winches and the traveler had to be through bolted. As Matthew stated, "The more we sailed,

Bernida

the more work we had to do. Our work list kept getting longer rather than shorter."

For Bob LaMere, sailing has played a big role in the life of his family. Sara and Al are sail makers, his son, David, graduated from the Great Lakes Maritime Academy. Another son, Daniel is a graduate from the University of Michigan in naval architecture. Bob has sailed in twenty five Mackinac races on both Lake Huron and Lake Michigan. He also did a transatlantic trip with his son David on a ninety foot sailboat named *Ondine*, one of the maxi racers of an earlier era. The trip was from Gibraltar in the Mediterranean to St. Thomas, VI, with a brief stop in the Canary Islands. Bob and his family spent their summers sailing all over the Great Lakes. In addition to his sailing skills, he is quite a craftsman. He built his own house fifty years ago. It is still the family home.

He had heard that *Bernida* was being restored up on Mackinac Island. Later, Sara told him that Al bought *Bernida* and planned to race her in the Bayview Mackinac Race in 2012. Bob said, "What in the world?" Like everyone else, Bob couldn't believe Al would attempt a Mackinac Race in a ninety one year old boat. Bob thought Al was crazy and honestly didn't think it could be done.

Nevertheless, Bob and Matthew began working on the boat together. Bob could see that the boat was not originally designed for blocks and all the other gear that would make it competitive. Bob had just recently remodeled his fifty year old home and had plenty of scrap wood left over. So, he brought the scraps down to the Bayview Yacht Club where the boat was being updated and went to work. As Bob would later say, "I've got a lot of my house in that boat." The grandson and grandpa made a very good partnership while working on the boat.

Matthew learned from Bob, and Bob was amazed at Matthew's problem solving skills and craftsmanship. Bob's passion for *Bernida* and the project grew daily.

The next step was to add a manual gusher pump, similar to the ones found on an Etchells, and a high capacity electric pump that would be powered by a mini Honda generator. If we can't keep the water out, we need a good method to get rid of it.

On April 8th, we began fairing the lead keel. We hired Dean Kuhn to do this. The forward portion of the keel had plenty of dents and scratches that needed to be addressed. It looked like Bernida had run aground numerous times and her keel had the scars to prove it. In addition to repairing the damage, we used this as an opportunity to fill some of the low spots and sand down some of the high spots. We probably should have spent more time fairing the keel than we did. Given the length of our work list, the job we did do was going to have to be good enough.

Dean Kuhn was another highly skilled craftsman Al enlisted to put *Bernida* in racing condition. He comes from a long line of ship builders beginning with his great grandfather. Dean still has some of his original chisels and hammers used to build sailboats. In 1990, Dean bought a boatyard at the mouth of the Detroit River and has been restoring old boats there for twenty two years. It was a time consuming task to fair the whole keel which was out of shape. He then stripped the keel down and filled in the bad spots. He also replaced a section of the stem near the bow.

Finally, after countless hours of work, *Bernida* was launched on May 10th. Many Bayview members came down to the crane to watch. When she went in, water poured into the boat everywhere. Everyone knew that the wood had to swell because

Bernida

she had been out of the water for a long time. Nonetheless, it was a bit disconcerting to see so much water coming in. Sara remembered being concerned about the boat filling with water during some of the early spring rain falls and going down to Bayview with Matthew to bail out the boat. Much to their surprise, the water had drained out on its own. So, launch day was huge! *Bernida* sat in the slings for a couple days. She was filled with water and we prayed she didn't sink. Al, Sara and Matthew were in California that weekend to watch Allison compete in the PAC 12 Rowing Championships. After a couple days, the slings were removed and *Bernida* floated! Sara recalls Al getting off the phone with Dock Master, Angelo Parisi, and telling Sara that *Bernida* was off life support and ready to go sailing upon their return home. All and all, it was a victorious weekend. Cal won the Pac 12 Women's Rowing Championships

Bernida Being Launched at Bayview Yacht Club.
Photo by Sara Declercq.

and *Bernida* floated.

On May 16th, we had our first sail out of Bayview with the updated rig in approximately 6 to 8 knots of wind. This was a photo shoot for the Grosse Pointe magazine. The boat was barely ready to sail. We sailed in the Detroit River for two hours. None of the winches had been installed and we had a make-shift running backstay system. We did get an opportunity to look at the main and see how the luff curve matched the bend in the mast. Prior to our next sail, we re-worked the mainsail adding shape to the upper quarter and reducing the luff curve in the lower quarter. We confirmed we would need three new winches in addition to the two winches we had already installed. With two weeks left before our first race, we had another long list of work that needed to be completed. This day was almost the end of the Bernida comeback story. *Bernida* had been assigned a well in the west harbor that theoretically should have been an easy well to sail in and out of. As we entered the harbor under main alone, it became apparent that we were going way too fast and would not be able to come to a stop in time. I quickly pushed the helm hard over just before *Bernida* entered her well. The plan was to make a 180° turn and exit the harbor and try another approach. Unfortunately I underestimated the turning radius. *Bernida* was headed right for the steel sea wall. Uniformly the entire crew yelled "WHAT ARE YOU DOING!" The partially lowered mainsail blocked most of my vision so I could not see the end of the sea wall. All I could see was the bow arcing to the left and the sea wall getting closer. At this point all we could do was hope we cleared the south end of the seawall. We cleared the seawall with only two feet to spare and our season was not ended by my lack of experience with the boat. In addition to a large turning radius,

Bernida coasts forever after dropping the sails. After dodging this bullet, we should have known then that someone would be looking out for Bernida this season.

Matthew and Bob continued to work daily on the long list of tasks. Allison was back from the NCAA Women's Rowing Championship, where her team and her boat finished third. She had one week at home before she left for her study abroad in Europe and wanted to help, so she worked for that week with her brother and grandpa. The extra set of hands was greatly appreciated by everyone.

The next event on our training schedule was the BYC One Design Regatta on June 6th. We sailed a portion of one race on Saturday. We sailed out to the starting line on a spinnaker run in around 18 knots of wind. Water was flowing unrestricted up the rudder post and through a crack in the transom. Fred looked at the rudder post as Matthew flipped the switch on the bilge pump and calmly said "I guess we know what the first item on our work list is." This gave us a good opportunity to evaluate our new running backstay system. As the spectra top mast backstay stretched, allowing the mast to bend too far forward for comfort, we would jibe to take the load off the running back stays. Then we would re-tension the spectra runners and jibe back to evaluate the tension on each of the three runners. After several jibes, we were happy with the balance between the three lines and felt we could safely sail downwind. Our running back stay system supported the mast in three places. The top support stay is connected to the top of the mast. The middle support connects to the mast approximately three quarters of the way up and supported the head stay. The bottom support line connected to the mast half way between the head stay and the boom and controlled the amount of mast bend in the lower half of the

*Bernida First Sail on the Detroit River.
Photo by Sara Declercq.*

*Safely in the Well After Almost Hitting the Seawall.
Photo by Matthew Declercq.*

mast. This is a sophisticated, but necessary, method to support the mast. We arrived at the starting area approximately fifteen minutes before the start. As we reached back and forth along the starting line, many of our competitors and the boats sailing in other classes shouted words of encouragement. We had one reef in the main and our smallest jib up. We wondered about the wisdom of testing Bernida in this much wind but all of us were excited to see how she would perform. As it usually does, our enthusiasm to race took precedence over a more rational decision to head home and test Bernida in a safer condition.

We had a good start at the leeward end of the starting line in clean air and Bernida was moving nicely to weather. One by one our competitors began to tack on to port tack and head towards the right side of the race course. We continued to sail on starboard tack towards the left side of the course. When we were most of the way out to the port lay line, the wind shifted to the left fifteen degrees and increased in velocity to 20 knots. This was excellent timing for Bernida. The shift in our favor put us into the lead and we tacked on to port tack to capitalize on the favorable shift and consolidate with the fleet. By then our starboard shrouds had stretched almost an inch and it was no longer safe to sail on starboard tack anyway. As we sailed toward the first mark on the port tack lay line, we re-tensioned the leeward shrouds that were visibly loose and shaking in the wind. By the time we arrived at the weather mark, the port shrouds had stretched to the point where it was not safe to sail on port anymore. In spite of the giant wind shift in our favor that would have put us two minutes ahead of the fleet at the first mark if we were sailing against similar boats, we rounded the mark in sixth place because our competitors were all bigger

Sailing Home from Bayview One Design Regatta.
Photo by Karen Hollerbach.

and faster boats. That being said we were very happy with Bernida's performance in heavy air. We made the decision to drop out of the race at the first mark and attend to our shrouds that had stretched past the point where we believed they would adequately support the mast. We sailed downwind for fifteen minutes and adjusted our shroud tension. When this was completed we put the boat back up on the wind and began to sail eight miles up wind back to Bayview in 20 knots of breeze.

Bernida

> This turned out to be an excellent test and we identified a number of areas that would require additional support. As we entered the mouth of the Detroit River, the wind was gusting up to 25 knots and we were pretty nervous about whether *Bernida* would hold up. We were very fortunate that the waves were small and successfully sailed her back to Bayview. Had we been sailing in similar winds in Lake Huron, the waves would have been substantially bigger and we may well have broken the mast or sustained major damage to the hull. Once we were tied up at the dock, we realized that we were lucky to get *Bernida* home and began to assess the damage to the boat. After stowing *Bernida's* sails and gear the crew headed up to the club for lunch. All of us were convinced that although we had lots of work to get done prior to the Mackinac race, we would be able to get *Bernida* race ready in time. We had a very upbeat crew debriefing and updated our work list again. The smiles were ear to ear and the trash talking had begun. We actually believed then that we could win the race!

Bob LaMere saw the condition of *Bernida* after Al and crew returned from the race. It had been a heavy weather race and the boat looked like it. There was definitely some structural damage which called for more lumber and more screws. The work list grew again.

> The steering system was all but destroyed. The aft section of the hull was bending up to the point that we were very close to breaking it off from the rest of the boat. The area between the turning block for the jib sheet and the cabin house winches had compressed and buckled the deck. The port spreader bracket had failed and the screws were pulling out of the mast. The starboard lower spreader bracket had begun to fail as well. It was very apparent that all of these issues would need to be

addressed if we had a reasonable expectation of completing the Mackinac race. With two weeks to go before our next scheduled race, we had lots of work to get done. We removed the mast and pulled Bernida out of the water to inspect the hull and rudder. The decision was made to hire veteran wood boat specialist Dean Kuhn to install a new rudder tube, rudder shaft, rudder bearings, and brackets to attach the rudder post. The 91 year old wood portion appeared in good condition so we left it in place and just replaced the rudder hardware. In an attempt to discover why the aft portion of the boat was bending up, we began the process of tapping the entire hull with a mallet looking for rotten wood. Strong wood would result in a clear pinging sound. Rotted wood will have a muffled dull sound. We discovered two sections of wood in the aft portion of the boat that needed to be replaced. In addition we discovered a two foot section of the center plank near the bow that was rotted as well. This was a fortunate discovery because it could have lead to a failure in the race. Dean Kuhn replaced the bad sections of wood along with the aging rudder parts and put a fresh coat of bottom paint on.

When Dean Kuhn first saw *Bernida*, Matthew and his grandpa Bob had already installed winches. They, in effect, had supercharged the boat. Dean felt the boat would require greater support of the deck in order to take the load it was never designed to handle. Dean installed a new rudder shaft because the original brass shaft was broken in the middle. He also added a shoe on the bottom of the new rudder shaft so that it wouldn't move around under a load. It still had its original white oak rudder.

Another one of his repairs on *Bernida* required him to laminate a block of solid oak which was staggered up and down in different directions. He hoped the wind would be suited to the boat's strength which was sailing off the wind because there was no cockpit coming. Although he would not be allowed to alter the boat's original design, he would have liked to laminate the coming to prevent water from filling the deep cockpit. He spent 100 hours working on the boat.

New Rudder Post & Support Block. Photo by Al Declercq.

While Dean was working on his list, Matthew Declercq and his grandpa added additional reinforcement to support the areas that failed on our heavy air beat and installed a winch for the mainsail and a mainsail traveler. Once this was complete, they installed an additional bilge pump and several pad eyes to allow the crew to precisely trim the sails. Matthew and Bob put in some long hours over a two week period and had *Bernida* ready to sail in the next regatta on her training schedule. While Matthew and Bob were working on the hull, Al worked with Todd Jones to redesign the spreader bracket angle and strengthen the attachment method.

June 16th was the date of the Detroit Yacht Club Classic Boat Regatta. In addition to a lot of fun, this regatta gave us an opportunity to sail against John Tipp's Yare. Yare is a Sparkman and Stevens 36 built in the1960's and has generally been the boat to beat in her Mackinac class over the years. She would serve as a bench mark for the progress we had made and help us discover how competitive we would be. Albacore, an S&S Pilot built in the 1940's was in our class as well. Albacore, Chippewa and Yare have been the top boats in the class that Bernida would be competing in the Mackinac Race and we could not wait to see how we stacked up. The class also included two NY 32's, Apache and Saphaifer. Sixteen boats in total were in our class. The race started at the mouth of the Detroit River off the Grosse Pointe Park Marina and the first mark was set three miles north of the start. The boats would round the first mark and head back to the Detroit River and finish off of the Detroit Yacht Club on Belle Isle.

I injured my hand a couple weeks earlier so Ward Detwiler helmed the boat at the start.

Ward Detwiler grew up sailing at Bayview from age seven. He attended high school at St. George's School in Newport Rhode Island where he sailed six days each week from March to June. Later, as a student at Northwestern University, he sailed six days a week on Lake Michigan. His sailing repertoire is quite complete, including numerous Chicago and Port Huron Mackinac Races, Newport to Bermuda and Transpac races. Many of these races were with his dad, Fred, Ken Flaska, Al Declercq and David LaMere. He is now twenty eight years old.

Bernida

Al told him about *Bernida* while sitting in the Bayview bar with Ken in June of 2011. He had this crazy idea to buy this old boat and win the Mackinac Race in 2012. After a couple beers, it sounded like a great idea.

Ward got a perfect start at the offshore end of the starting line. Bernida was up to full speed and right on time when the starting gun went off. We had our largest genoa up and were headed right at the first mark with the wind just forward of our beam. The next boat to cross the starting line was almost three boat lengths behind us. By then we had hoisted a Code Zero asymmetrical spinnaker that we had borrowed from Chuck Bayer off of his Beneteau 36.7. Bernida performed beautifully with this borrowed sail. Two minutes into the race, I looked

Start of Detroit Yacht Club Classic Boat Regatta.
Photo by Chris Clark.

Bernida

at the crew and said we would be building a Code Zero for the Mackinac race. It was very clear that Bernida loved this sail and we would have to have one. Ward accused me of just wanting to have another pillow to sleep on during the Mackinac race. Matthew was in favor of the new sail because he figured if I got another pillow, then he did too. Shortly after the start we had worked our way into a nice lead of a couple hundred yards and were feeling pretty good about our chances to win the race. Then Yare began to catch us. Yare was slightly faster than us on this point of sail and began to narrow the gap. By the first mark, Yare was only ten boat lengths behind. We made the decision to drop our Code Zero asymmetrical spinnaker as we approached the mark and put up our genoa. As we jibed around the first mark and headed back towards the finish line, the wind angle was perfect for our genoa. Yare elected to jibe their asymmetrical, rather than change to her genoa at the mark. The wind was too far forward for her asymmetrical and we began to extend our lead again. By the time Yare doused her asymmetrical and set her genoa, we had a comfortable lead again.

   Once we both had the same sail combination, Yare began to show her speed again. Slowly but surely she was catching us. Apache, the fastest boat in the fleet was catching us as well. We knew we could never hold off Apache but we thought if we continued to work hard, we could hold off Yare. About the time we were two miles from the finish line, Apache sailed over the top of us. It was a beautiful sight. She had her big genoa up and was healed over going as fast as the old girl goes. The boom was dragging in the water and her crew comprised mostly of the Gmeiner family members were grinning from ear to ear. Apache is a magnificent boat. About a mile from the finish line, Yare had clawed her way back into the race and was only a few boat lengths behind us. We expected a real battle to the finish line.

Just off of the Bayview Yacht Club, the wind started to shift to the left and free us up. The crew quickly set our Code Zero again and immediately we jumped a knot in speed. We had beaten Yare to the punch and were extending our lead again. Shortly after we set our Code Zero, Yare set hers but it was too late. We were only a half mile from the finish line and although she was going slightly faster, there just wasn't enough race course left for her to catch us. Apache finished first. We finished second and Yare finished third. With our handicap, we corrected over Apache and won the race. Our crew was ecstatic, yet at the same time we knew that we had plenty of work to do if we expected to win the Mackinac race. Long time friends Jay Schmidt and Mike Napa had filled in for Ken and Connor. After the race our crew, joined by Sara and Allison, drove over to the Detroit Yacht Club for the awards party. It was lots of fun talking with the crews of the other boats. It was evident that all the competitors were rooting for Bernida to have a successful Mackinac race. After all, a win for one classic boat would be a victory for every classic boat.

The Grosse Point Sail Club Regatta was held on June 30th. We didn't plan on racing this day. We had completed most of our work list from the debriefing after the Classic Boat Regatta and wanted to test several improvements we had made and take a look at the new masthead spinnaker and A-3 reaching asymmetrical. We left Bavyiew around ten in the morning and began to sail up the Detroit River towards Lake St. Clair.

Once we had all of our sheets lead and equipment in place, we hoisted our new asymmetrical spinnaker. The sail looked great and Bernida took off. It was apparent that we had some more

Apache & Bernida in Detroit Yacht Club Classic Boat Regatta. Photo by Chris Clark.

work to do on our mast tuning. The tip of the mast was falling way too far off to leeward for comfort and we would need more tension on our diamond stays prior to using this sail again. We did not want to take any chances so we dropped this sail and continued sailing out into the lake under headsail.

When we reached the lake and had enough room to bear off and set our new masthead spinnaker, Bernida went from 4.5 knots to 6 knots and was perfectly balanced. The new rudder system felt very solid and we only had a few drops of water coming out of the top of the rudder shaft tube. We all looked at each other and concurred that if we could get a few hours of these conditions in the Mackinac race, we would be hard to beat.

Bernida

We were approaching the race area for the Grosse Point Sail Club regatta and I asked the guys if they wanted to race. Everyone was up for it so we hoisted our jib and dropped our spinnaker. This crew cannot pass up a good competition. We arrived at the starting line just as the starting gun went off. As a result of our poor start we spent most of the first leg of the race sailing in bad air in the wind shadow of our competitors. At the first mark we were in sixth place, approximately two minutes behind the leaders. The boats that rounded ahead of us all set their spinnakers and sailed a course almost directly at the next mark. We could see that there was a nice puff of wind coming in from the right side of the course so we elected to sail a course that was approximately fifteen degrees higher than the course to the next mark. When the puff reached us we started to catch the fleet ahead of us.

All of the boats ahead of us were in a pack sitting on each others' air and preventing each other from pushing down in the puffs and heating the boat up in the lulls. We were all by ourselves in the most pressure on the far right. We had more pressure and could work the boat with no limitations. So, as a result, we gained more than a minute on this leg and found ourselves very close to the fleet as we approached the second mark. The crew did a terrific job getting our jib up and dousing the spinnaker. We were able to cut across the transoms and inside of two boats and moved ourselves into third place at the mark. Because the wind had been much stronger on the right hand side of the run, we wanted to get to the left on the beat up to the third mark. We tacked onto starboard and sailed for a couple hundred yards. Zubenelgenubi had taken a tack to the left as well and we were the two furthest boats to the left. Albacore had continued to sail on port tack off to the right. As it turned out, we and Zubenelgenubi had made the right choice.

The wind shifted twenty degrees to the left and increased in velocity. We both tacked and sailed for a substantial amount of time on port tack, with Zubenelgenubi approximately 100 yards to weather. I don't think either one of us gained an inch over ten minutes. While Albacore was barely moving, we were headed almost right at the mark and going 5.5 knots.

Both of us had done well on this leg and arrived at the third mark with a very comfortable lead. We were able to gain approximately one minute on the run to the finish line, where we crossed the line in first place. Our assessment after this race was that we were just another boat on the race course while sailing upwind, but downwind Bernida would be special. That evening most of the crew would be attending the annual Bayview Summer Party and after a stellar day of sailing, we were looking forward to the event. Most of the conversation at the party revolved around how far Bernida would make it up the Michigan shoreline before we had to drop out of the Mackinac race. Our crew was beginning to outwardly express our confidence and the typical response was not only could we finish the race; we could win if the conditions were moderate. As with all the previous races, each time we sailed Bernida, the crew came up with more ideas to improve our chances of winning. For the first time all of the items on the list weren't mandatory. Some would be luxuries. Matthew and Bob, with the help of the crew, spent the next week and a half completing the remaining items on our list. Ken came up with an innovative bracket that would allow us to attach a flashlight to the shrouds that we could focus on the jib while sailing at night. This turned out to be a big help Sunday night in the Mackinac race.

Bernida

The night before our tow to Pt Huron there were only a couple things left to do. We secured all the necessary parts and tools and loaded them on the boat. Bob and Matthew would have another busy day.

On Thursday, July 12th, two days before the Mackinac Race, *Bernida* was towed from the Bayview Yacht Club to the Port Huron Yacht Club by a long time friend of ours, Dane Christy.

Dane Christy is a Bayview member and the co-owner with Dave Lockhart of a Farr 49 racing boat named *Courtesan*. In the fall of 2011, he was approached by Al with the idea of restoring *Bernida* and racing her in the 2012 Bayview Mackinac Race. Dane thought it was an admirable idea, but a little crazy.

Dane, who is a builder, was involved in some of the discussions with the *Bernida* crew about improvements they were considering for the boat. Although on occasion they sought his advice, they didn't necessarily take it.

As the date for the July 14 start of the 2012 Bell's Beer Bayview Mackinac Race approached, Al asked Dane to tow *Bernida* from Bayview to the Port Huron Yacht Club two days before the race. They left at 7:00 AM. The trip through Lake St. Clair and the length of the St. Clair River took eleven hours. Matthew Declercq and his grandpa, Bob LaMere were aboard *Bernida*. Dane said the old wooden boat was leaking so much that they were pumping water out most of the way. Dane has owned wooden boats in the past and was not surprised to see *Bernida* leaking under a load.

The boat was towed from Bayview Yacht Club in the Detroit River across the entire length of Lake St. Clair and into the freighter channel of the St. Clair River. This route led to its eventual destination, The Port Huron Yacht Club located on the Black River in downtown Port Huron, Michigan. Matthew

Bernida

*Courtesan & Bernida at Bayview Yacht Club.
Photo by Julie Christy.*

*Courtesan Towing Bernida From Bayview Yacht Club to Port Huron.
Photo by Sara Declercq.*

Bernida

worked on projects all day and Bob steered the boat in the wake of *Courtesan*. They watched the guys on *Courtesan* drinking beers and eating sandwiches while sitting in comfortable chairs they had on the deck. The guys on *Courtesan* were able to switch drivers all day too. It was a hot day and Matthew and his grandpa were probably not as comfortable on *Bernida*. They had plenty of food and drinks, but they did not have chaise lounges and the ability to walk about.

Matthew Declercq & Al Declercq Installing Non-Skid on Foredeck. Photo by Sara Declercq.

On Friday night, Matthew stayed on the boat. He was performing last minute equipment checks. He also wanted to keep people off the boat. He poured his heart and soul into this project and he was not going to let anything happen to *Bernida* now. He went to sleep at 2:00AM Saturday morning after lining the sea stove with tin foil so they wouldn't burn down the boat once they were underway. He slept 4½ hours until 6:30AM. After the months of labor, numerous repairs and the sea trials in heavy weather, Matthew felt with 100% certainty that the boat was ready.

It was July 14, 2012, race day. The crew on *Bernida* would be three fathers and three sons; Al and Matthew Declercq, Ken and Connor Flaska and Fred and Ward Detwiler.

Ken Flaska started sailing in high school and has competed in more than twenty five Mackinac races. Ken, Fred and Al have been sailing together since the mid 70's and have accumulated thousands of miles while yacht racing. Ken is a successful attorney in the Detroit area. He and his son Connor were excited about the idea of racing *Bernida* from the outset. Al came to them in the fall of 2011 to see if they wanted to sail with him on *Bernida* in the upcoming Bayview Mackinac race. He met with Ken at Bayview and showed them the placemat at the club that included the story of *Bernida*. Fred Detwiler was building a new boat which would not be finished until 2013. Since they were without a boat for 2012 and because it would be just fathers and sons, it sounded too good to pass up. It would definitely be something different. It created a lot of enthusiasm all summer leading up to the race. Ken kept getting texts and

At the Dock, Morning of the Race at Port Huron Yacht Club. Photo by Sara Declercq.

Bernida

*Leaving the Dock at the Port Huron Yacht Club.
Photo by Sara Declercq.*

emails from other sailors wishing him good luck. Lots of sailors were rooting for *Bernida* to win. Sara and Roxanne said they felt like celebrities walking around Pt. Huron. They were wearing *Bernida* shirts and got approached by all kinds of people asking about the boat. Both sailors and non-sailors said they came to Pt. Huron just to get a glimpse of the boat they had been reading about all summer.

  In her original configuration, *Bernida*'s equipment was very sparse. It had no main sheet or running backstay winch, which made them wonder how the 1925 guys got the boat all the way to Mackinac Island. Like Fred, Ken was out of town sailing in another regatta when *Bernida* sailed in the Classic Boat Regatta. He was on *Bernida* during the Bayview One Design Regatta and remembers water shooting up from the rudder post and many other places where water came in. He felt safer on the boat after they had a pump system installed. The spinnakers were large and they learned that light air downwind was the boat's sweet spot.

Like the other sons aboard *Bernida*, Connor Flaska learned how to sail at the Bayview Yacht Club junior sailing program. Beginning at age nine, he moved from the Opti to the Laser. He began sailing on the big boats with his dad, Ken, at age thirteen. Connor sailed his first Mackinac race with his dad in 2007. In the fall of 2011, Al and Ken sent him an email, while he was away at Curry College, inviting him to race on *Bernida*. They said they would become a part of history if they made this voyage. It was a slam dunk sale. He was in!

When Connor finally saw the boat, however, he thought, "We're gonna need a bigger one." He is convinced that they wouldn't have completed the race without all the work that Matthew and the other craftsmen put into it. He hoped that they wouldn't get a big blow in the middle of the night on this old boat with its deep cockpit.

Fred Detwiler and his wife Barbara have two sons, Ward and Bradley. Like many others mentioned in this book, this is a sailing family. Fred has raced all over the world and has built and owned many racing boats. All of his boats have been named *Trader* and have included a One Ton, an Andrews 70, and a Jim Donavan Transpac 52. He is currently building a carbon fiber, Bruce Nelson designed, custom 88 foot racer/cruiser which will be launched in 2013. He is planning to sail around the world on this, his latest boat named *Trader*. Al Declercq and Ken Flaska have crewed with him on many salt water and fresh water races over the years.

All his life, he has been a sailor beginning with his time

Bernida

Ken Flaska & Connor Flaska Early Sunday Evening in Mackinac Race. Photo by Al Declercq.

on his parents' boats. Ward, his older son, began racing with him at the age of nine on his first Mackinac Race. Ward has also done multiple Newport to Bermuda races with him.

In the fall of 2011, Al called Fred and told him he had purchased *Bernida*. He was getting it ready to enter in the 2012 Bayview Mackinac Race and wanted Fred and Ward to crew with him. Fred's initial response was, "You've got to be kidding." At the time Al called him, Ken and Connor Flaska, Al and Matthew and Ward were committed.

Fred's first thought was, "We've got to be sure that this boat can make it." Ward had to convince him to look at the boat more closely. Fred finally concluded that, with a lot of work, they could actually make it to Mackinac. All the crew began offering ideas on how best to rig the boat. Fred did not sail on *Bernida* in its initial race on the Detroit River because he was involved in the 2012 Newport to Bermuda Race on a boat with Gary Jobson aboard.

Fred and Ward both helped with rigging, but Matthew did most of the work. Fred was extremely impressed that Matthew could manage this whole project at the age of seventeen. There were no failures as a result of his work. Fred's wife, Barbara, wasn't quite sure about this boat and insisted that they have a chase boat to follow them the whole way.

On race day, Sara brought the final provisions for the boat. She checked the marine weather forecast and it seemed ideal. She felt they would be alright because they knew the limitations of the boat. She and Roxanne Flaska, whose husband, Ken and son, Connor were on *Bernida*, have an annual ritual of driving to Harbor Springs and staying overnight on race day. All through the day and into the night they were tracking the progress of *Bernida* on their computers and cell phones.

Roxanne Flaska, wife of Ken and mother of Connor, grew up in Maine. As a child, she loved being on the water. She spent most of her time on inland lakes on power boats. She has a great respect for the water and is very safety conscious when boating. She has been very supportive though of her husband Ken's lifelong passion for sailboat racing. That being said, she was concerned about this race.

Her son, Connor, also had become an avid and knowledgeable racer like his dad. Whenever he was in kids' regattas, she volunteered to help with the many details of running a regatta. She is always amazed at how sailors can remember every detail of every race they were ever in. As Roxanne puts it though, "I'm happy to see them happy doing what they love to do."

She was very nervous about them racing to Mackinac on *Bernida*. Ken told her that Al bought this old wooden boat,

Bernida

but she didn't realize how small it was until she saw it in a boat slip at the Bayview Yacht Club. The age of the boat as well as its small size was a concern because of the storms that can kick up on the Great Lakes. She kept asking herself, "How can these six big guys sail that far on such a small boat with no engine?" Another recent memory was on her mind as well. *Bernida*'s attempt would be one year after the drowning of two crew members aboard *Wing Nuts* in a storm during the Chicago Race to Mackinac in July of 2011.

    Barb Detwiler is the wife of Fred Detwiler and stepmother to Ward and Bradley. She owns her own accounting firm in Grosse Pointe. She was never into sailing until she met Fred. In the twenty years of their marriage, however, she has done many offshore sailing cruises aboard their own yachts. Their cruising destinations have included Mexico, the Caribbean and many other destinations.

    In the fall of 2011, Fred told her that Al Declercq purchased a ninety year old wooden sailboat that he intended to restore and race in the 2012 Bayview Mackinac Race. She immediately responded by telling him that the idea was nuts. She saw the boat once on Mackinac Island and thought it was too small for the big guys who would be together for two days and nights on Lake Huron. That thought did not change when she saw *Bernida* again upon her arrival at Bayview in December.

    Roxanne, who was very worried about the trip, felt a little better when she heard Barbara Detwiler say, "My husband is not racing on that boat." Upon hearing that, Roxanne thought, "Maybe that would be the end of it." Eventually, however, Barbara did relent with the promise that *Bernida* would have a chase boat follow her during the race in case they needed to abandon ship. Ken also gave Roxanne re-assurance that they were carrying a six man inflatable life raft and new high tech life jackets with transponders.

Barb did like the fact that they would be on the shore course in sight of land. She also had complete confidence in Fred who was a very experienced offshore sailor and a survivor of a hurricane at sea. In terms of the race itself, *Bernida's* experienced crew would make them tough to beat if they didn't have a mechanical breakdown.

So, there they were, Sara, Roxanne and Barb, their concerns temporarily put on hold, standing on the dock at the Port Huron Yacht Club on Saturday July 14, 2012 waving goodbye to their husbands and sons. As the crew shoved off, *Bernida's* daring attempt to repeat sailing history was now underway.

2012 BELL'S BEER BAYVIEW MACKINAC RACE-JULY 14, 2012

Bernida had no outboard or inboard motor and had to be towed to the starting line at the southern tip of Lake Huron. During this 1½ hour trip, Matthew was able to catch some more sleep below.

Gordy Smith was kind enough to tow us out to the start from the Pt. Huron Yacht Club. We left the dock at 10:00 AM Saturday morning. As we pushed off the dock we threw our anchor road, which was doubling as a tow line, to one of Gordy's crew. We secured our end of the line to the mast at the deck level. Then we tied two rolling hitches to the tow line and ran lines to the port and starboard cabin house winches to take a portion of the load. We had made it this far and the last thing we wanted to do was damage the boat on the way out to the start. Gordy took it easy as we headed out of the Black River and turned north for our journey up the St. Clair River. The river was filled with spectator boats and competitors heading out to the start and the shoreline was packed with spectators.

Shortly after we had passed under the Blue Water Bridge, my phone rang. It was Gordy. He said that this was probably the fastest we were going to go for three days. We laughed and I thanked him for the tow and asked him to slow down and cut us loose. Once we had slowed down, we hoisted the main and our big genoa and started sailing out to the starting area. The wind was out of the east at approximately 7 knots.

When we arrived at the starting area, a couple of the guys went for a quick swim to wash the waterline and then we had

Bernida Sail Inventory.
Photo by Al Declercq.

a quick crew meeting. Most of what we covered in this meeting, Fred, Ken and I have been through fifty times together. That being said we always take our pre-race meetings seriously. We discussed the weather forecast and how it should affect our strategy.

We reviewed the sail inventory and the conditions in which we should have each sail up. We talked about where our equipment and provisions were located below. We formalized our watch system, and we discussed crew safety. Matthew walked us through our electronics and in particular, how to operate our ICOM ASI personal locater system. Fred reviewed the operation of our satellite phone and how to arm our personal broadcaster units should anyone fall overboard. I went over the conditions in which we would wear our safety harnesses and life jackets and when we would hook into our jack lines.

Bernida presented some special safety concerns. We did not have an engine which meant we would need to sail our way out of any predicament we got ourselves into. We did not have life lines, so we would need to take extra caution to ensure that none of us fell overboard. These were small concerns compared to the risk of taking on more water than we could handle. The rest of the fleet all had self draining cockpits. As water flows into their cockpits, it exits the boat through a drain system and does not end up in the bilge. On Bernida, any water we took on ran straight into the bilge. Bernida is an open cockpit design with minimal freeboard. In rough conditions, we expected to take on a considerable amount of water. To combat this problem, Matthew and Bob LaMere installed three new bilge pumps. The first was a large manual gusher pump. This would be our pump of last resort other than buckets, and had the capacity we believed was necessary to keep *Bernida* afloat in an emergency. In addition Matthew and Bob installed two electric bilge pumps. The first was a conventional 750 gallon per hour pump that would be our primary pump. The second was a 4000 gallon per hour pump that we would only use in the most severe conditions. Both of these pumps ran off of a battery and we used a small Honda generator to charge the battery.

In early July, Al tested the pump system while *Bernida* was in the well at Bayview. He put a hose in the boat and opened the valve. The water poured in for two hours until the water level reached the seats. With the boat almost full of water, *Bernida's* deck was six inches from the water. Al turned off the water and turned the electric bilge pump on. It only took twenty minutes to pump *Bernida* dry.

Our start was scheduled for 12:00. The class starting before us was Cruising "C" with a scheduled start time of 11:50. While we were sailing around the starting area, the wind velocity and direction were constantly shifting. When the wind would back to the left, it looked like the Code Zero would be the best sail to start with. When it was in a right phase, the A-3 Asymmetrical would be the correct sail. We hoisted both sails and determined the break even wind direction for the two sails.

Our original plan was to start at the inshore, or leeward, end of the starting line. We believed that the wind velocity would be stronger along the Michigan shore for the first couple hours of the race and wanted to be the closest boat to the Michigan shore at the start. We were also concerned that if we ended up in a luffing match with one or more of our competitors that all of us would end up sailing higher than necessary and as a result, we would end up further off shore than we wanted to be. We watched the Cruising "C" start and the boats that started

Bernida Pre-Race

at the inshore end were able to get off the starting line cleanly and aim straight up the rum line to Harbor Beach. The boats at the weather end ended up sailing significantly higher than we wanted to sail. So with five minutes to go before our start, we confirmed our decision to start at the inshore end. We had our jib up and had rigged the A-3 Asymmetrical so we were ready to set the sail as the starting gun was fired.

At four minutes before the start, we were at the inshore end of the starting line headed away from the starting line. Fred Detwiler looked up to weather and saw a giant puff rolling in from the east. He yelled, "There is a good breeze coming in from the east." We immediately tacked the boat and started to head towards the offshore end of the starting line. We had to sail hard on the wind to get to the weather end of the line. This was a drastic departure from our game plan, but we all agreed

Bernida

that this represented a great opportunity to get a jump on our class at the start. With a minute and a half to go, we were half way up the long starting line and it was becoming more apparent we had made the right choice. Because the breeze was increasing, we expected to be going faster at the start which would drive our apparent wind direction further forward. We made the decision to switch from the A-3 all purpose reaching Asymmetrical to our close reaching Code Zero asymmetrical. Ken, Matthew and Conner scampered to get the sheets and tack line off the A-3 and connected them to the Code Zero. With fifteen seconds to spare, we got the Code Zero hooked up and we hoisted the sail. By then we were at the weather end of the line and the Code Zero filled as the starting gun went off. Our adrenalin was up! After months of hard work, we were finally racing Bernida to Mackinac!

We started just to windward of Bob Wall's Chippewa and

Four Minutes Before the Start of the Race

were the closest boat to the committee boat. Our end of the line had 8 knots of wind and our competitors in the middle of the line and inshore end were sailing in 6 knots of wind. This gave Chippewa and us a big edge over the fleet. Chippewa chose to start the race with their genoa rather than going with a spinnaker right away. This decision allowed them to sail higher, or closer to the wind, than us, and in sailing, the leeward boat has the right-of-way over the windward boat. Chippewa used this rule to their advantage and attempted to make us sail higher than we could carry the Code Zero. Just as they were getting close to us, we sailed over the top of them and broke clear ahead. We had the correct sail up for the conditions, going a full knot faster than Chippewa, and began to pull away from her. Chippewa immediately switched to a spinnaker, but the wind was too far forward for a conventional spinnaker and she steadily fell back. Other favorites, Wind Stalker, Albacore, Camelot, and Zubenelgenubi were all sailing in lighter breeze in the middle of the line. Thanks to Fred's last minute call, we started at the correct end of the line in more breeze than our competitors. We had made the perfect sail selection for the conditions and were sailing straight at our desired waypoint located 2 miles off Harbor Beach. Five minutes into the race, we were one minute ahead of the closest boat in our class. Over the next hour, we extended our lead to almost a mile over the second place boat, Camelot. The "youth movement" as we affectionately referred to Matthew, Connor and Ward were focused and doing an outstanding job of sailing Bernida. It is difficult to describe the pride that Fred, Ken and I had seeing the great sailors our sons had become. It was now apparent they were taking us for a ride to Mackinac; a true changing of the guard.

Bernida

Two hours into the race we heard a loud noise. The block at the masthead that the Code Zero halyard was run through broke. The halyard had jammed between the containing edge of the block and the sheave. It was only a matter of time before the block would fail completely and our sail would fall down into the water. At this point we could not lower the sail because the halyard was jammed in the block. The decision was made to send a man to the top of the mast using a second halyard.

Ken said, "We've got to go up." Since Ken was the lightest crew member on the boat, he was chosen to go up the rig. He quickly put the boat's climbing harness on and grabbed a spare block and the tools he thought he would need to fix the problem. We attached the second halyard on to Ken's harness and began to pull him to the top of the mast. Matthew and Ward pulled on the halyard at the mast while Al and Conner wound the halyard around the cabin house winch and took up the slack. About the time Ken was half way to the top of the mast, the second mast head block that was supporting Ken exploded. Luckily Ken was hanging on to the mast at the time and this did not result in a serious accident. Two hours into the race, both of our mast head blocks were destroyed and we had 190 miles left to the finish line. This was not the way we wanted to start the race. We lowered Ken back down to the deck in order to assess our options. We came too far for this journey to end now. Just then the halyard the Code Zero was set on broke through the block and our Code Zero came most of the way down. We quickly gathered in the sail without damaging it. This wasn't a good situation either and we knew our competition would be cutting into our lead if we did not act quickly. We had one small spinnaker in our inventory that we hoisted on a lower halyard that only went three quarters of the way to the top. This

L to R: Matthew, Connor & Ward (The Youth Movement). Photo by Sara Declercq.

fractional sail was designed for heavy winds and was set just above the head stay. Although this was not the perfect sail for the conditions, it was better than not having any sail up.

Once this sail was set, we lowered the mainsail to the deck. The mainsail halyard was the only operational halyard we had left that went all the way to the top of the mast. We connected the mainsail halyard to Ken's climbing harness and started to raise him to the top of the mast. As it turns out, the mainsail block was the original brass block built in 1921. I asked Ken if he wanted me, as the captain, to perform last rights before he went up to the top of the rig supported by a ninety year old sheave and shackle. The crew all laughed and tossed in a few comments of their own. We knew this was a serious situation, but we did not let it get us down. This was our last chance. If this failed we wouldn't be able to set any of our masthead spinnakers for the remainder of the race and perhaps we would not be able to hoist the mainsail again. The good news is that the 91 year old mainsail halyard sheave didn't fail and we were able to hoist Ken to the top of the rig. Ken replaced the two broken blocks with our spare blocks and re-ran the halyards through them. This was not nearly as easy as it might sound.

Ken had to unscrew the shackle pins that attach the blocks to the mast without dropping them and then screw them back in. Ken was close to fifty feet off the water and was swinging back and forth like a pendulum. The wood mast was bending and shaking throughout the repair. Just imagine a tree blowing in the wind. I, as is the custom when we sail together, was making fun of him and asking if he was having a good time. The rest of the crew had their fair share of barbs as well. Fred did an excellent job of focusing on driving the boat through this repair, making Ken's ride as smooth as possible.

Ken was able to make the repairs and we lowered him back down to the deck. Once Ken was down, we reattached the mainsail halyard to the main and raised the mainsail back to the top of the mast. Now all we had to do was lower our undersized fractional spinnaker that we had temporarily set and raise the Code Zero back up. All of this took less than fifteen minutes but it seemed like an eternity. In situations like this one, it is great to be able to draw on years of experience. Ken and the crew did a great job of working us out of this predicament and we were back sailing at full speed towards Harbor Beach. We were very fortunate that we had two spare blocks on the boat, and a crew that was up to the task.

Code Zero Asymmetrical spinnakers are the closest reaching legal spinnakers allowed by the PHRF rule that we were competing under. The sail is a cross between a genoa and a spinnaker. The luff, or forward edge of the sail, is designed so that when fully tensioned, it stretches from the top of the mast to the deck at the bow. The leech, or trailing edge of the sail, is shorter than the luff. The rule allows the combination of an asymmetrical spinnaker's luff and leech to be the same length as the luff and the leech of a conventional spinnaker. So every foot

Sailing with Code Zero Shortly After the Start—Photo by BoatPIX.

that you add to the front of the sail, you need to deduct from the trailing edge of the sail. The foot, or bottom edge of the sail, is the same length as a conventional spinnaker. The measurement from luff to leech half way up the sail must be a minimum of 75% of the foot length to be considered a spinnaker. This is a specialty sail designed to be used when the wind direction is between forty-five and eighty degrees off the bow. For the first five hours of the race, this was the perfect sail for the wind conditions. Without this sail, we would have been just another boat in the race rather than the fastest boat in our class.

Approximately 30 miles into the race, the wind started to strengthen a little and clock to the southeast. This meant that the Code Zero was no longer the perfect sail for the conditions so we dropped this sail and hoisted our A-3 reaching asymmetrical spinnaker. Once again, we benefited from having

Navigation Station.
Photo by Matthew Declercq.

the perfect sail for the conditions and continued to extend our lead. Within a few hours, we had extended our lead to almost 6 miles. By now all of us had taken a turn at the helm and we were beginning to feel very comfortable with Bernida.

Dane Christy, who towed *Bernida* from the Bayview Yacht Club to Port Huron, stayed up in Port Huron because he was entered in the PRHF B Class and would be racing on the longer course to Cove Island in the Mackinac Race. It was an easy race for his Farr 49. When they reached the tip of the thumb, they made directly for Cove Island. Even though competing boats may be on the same race course, they often experience differing weather conditions. This was especially the case for Dane and his boat, *Courtesan*. An isolated squall hit the boat with 22 knots of wind speed which persisted for three hours. Because his boat was the only boat in his class caught in the squall, those three hours gave him great separation from his competitors. Dane won his class and reached Mackinac Island just after dark Sunday night. Shortly after finishing, the breeze died which delayed the arrival of the other boats in his class. He thinks the isolated squall was the biggest factor that helped him win. Al told him the good karma he gained towing *Bernida* to Port Huron won the race for him.

Around 8:00PM Saturday night, we were just north of Harbor Beach and our new waypoint was Thunder Bay light. The winds began to clock further to the south and it was time to switch from our A-3 to a conventional spinnaker. We made the change just in time as the wind continued to clock and once again had the perfect sail up for the conditions. So far everything was going according to our plan and the conditions were perfect for Bernida. We used this sail all night as we lead the fleet toward the Island.

> *Our game plan was to stay approximately 12 miles offshore through the night. Our weather forecast called for stronger winds 12-15 miles off shore than they would be closer to the Michigan shoreline. We were a little closer to the Michigan shore than we wanted to be, but the wind velocity was higher than we expected it to be and we felt comfortable with our position. We knew that if the wind velocity stayed up for another hour, the northern tip of the thumb of Michigan would be abeam and the shore line would fall off quickly as we began to cross Saginaw Bay.*
>
> *This was a great night to sail. The wind direction was oscillating back and forth twenty degrees. When the wind would back to the southeast, we would sail on starboard. When the wind direction would clock to the south we would jibe onto a port tack. We must have jibed eight to ten times during the night. Each time we would jibe when the wind shifted and we were able to sail directly at our waypoint, one mile off Thunder Bay Light, all night long.*

Keeping with their twenty year tradition, Roxanne and Sara drove up to Harbor Springs to stay Saturday night. Sara said it was a restless night for her, because her mind was with Al and Matthew. Sara did fall off to sleep with *Bernida* foremost on her mind. She was dreaming she was racing on *Bernida*. A storm came through Harbor Springs and a lightning bolt struck a tree just outside her hotel room. As she related later, "It was the loudest sound I ever heard. Because I was dreaming that I was on *Bernida*, I jumped out of bed thinking the boat's mast was coming down. After that, I went back to tracking the boat. I prayed that the storm would not make it over to Lake Huron."

These were challenging conditions to sail in. When the wind is out of the southern quadrants in the Great Lakes, the conditions

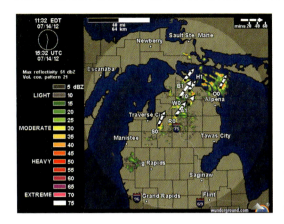

Weather Download on Al Declercq's Cell Phone.

are always cloudy. Wispy clouds form, limiting any lighting effect from the moon. With no light from the moon, and all the stars blocked, there was nothing to steer on. Sailing dead downwind with only the angle to the waves and the compass to steer by is quite difficult. Compounding the challenge is Bernida's running lights that were only a foot and a half off the water. They reflected off the water and created a green and red haze, making it virtually impossible to see anything. If we were steering a little higher than the ideal course, the boat began to heal a little bit and we could feel the acceleration. If we were a little lower than the desired course, the spinnaker trimmer would alert the helmsman that the wind was too far aft and we were close to jibing. The spinnaker trimmer's input was the key to success in these conditions. Matthew and Ward took advantage of their young eyes and great night vision and excelled. Conner worked the spinnaker sheet aggressively and constantly provided feedback to the helmsman. Our team work was terrific and we were sailing Bernida to her maximum potential. Once again, the "youth movement" showed us they had arrived!

Bernida

> *Around 8:00AM Sunday morning, we sighted Jon Somes's J44, Sagitta, and Ray Adam's Beneteau 42, Epic, approximately one mile to the west of us on our beam. We had continued to lead the fleet all night long and felt very good about our chances to win the race. By then we had covered over 122 miles and were closing in on Thunder Bay.*
>
> *All of us expected the bigger and faster boats on our course to start passing us by 6:00PM Saturday evening. To still be the lead boat in the fleet at 8:00AM Sunday morning was way beyond our expectations. We had lost cell phone coverage for a while and were not able to track our competitors online for a few hours. We were a little nervous about our lead. We knew that most of our class was faster than us in these conditions and we expected to discover that our lead had disappeared through the night. Seeing Epic and Sagitta, which are much larger and faster boats in another class, confirmed that we had a great night and it eased our concerns. I never remember a night of sailing when every time we jibed or tacked it turned out to be the correct decision. It was as if God was looking over Bernida and winning a third Mackinac race was her destiny.*

During the race, David LaMere, Sara's brother, was a crewman aboard *Talisman*, a 58 foot custom design racer owned by Bruce Aitken. Bruce is a long time friend of Al, Ken and Fred and has sailed thousands of miles with them. *Talisman* was on the longer Cove Island course to the Island. Because the largest boats are the last to start the race, David did get a chance to see *Bernida* go off with its competitors. He was excited to see her grab a commanding lead from the starting gun. Later, he would periodically log onto his boat's race tracker to see how *Bernida* was performing while working her way up the shore course. Like most of the boats on the Cove Island course, the *Talisman* crew was rooting for *Bernida* to win.

On Sunday morning, Sara and Roxanne drove up from Harbor Springs to Mackinaw City and took the ferry to the Island. It's always fun for them to be on the Island because they have so many friends who are awaiting the arrival of the racers when the fleet begins arriving Sunday evening.

On Sunday afternoon Roxanne was down on the docks and noticed that the boat designated as the chase boat for *Bernida* was sitting in a boat well. Very alarmed, she came up to the boat owner and asked, "What are you doing here? You are supposed to be following *Bernida*!" He told her that, when the crew reached Harbor Beach, they called and said they wouldn't need his help anymore. She became very upset with this news because the chase boat was something that *Bernida* could no longer rely on in an emergency. Roxanne did not realize that Gary Marowski, the owner of the chase boat was tracking *Bernida* and had told the crew that he was only a phone call away if they needed him.

The wind had dropped in velocity to approximately six knots and was oscillating between east and south. When the wind would switch to the east, we would put the A-3 up. When it would shift back to the south, we would go back to our spinnaker. Throughout the day we must have switched sails a dozen times. For a while off of Presque Isle Light, the wind went very light around 4:00PM in the afternoon. We switched to our wind seeker and were only able to sail at a half mile to a mile an hour. We weren't making much progress but at least we were moving. In long distance races you always worry when you come to a stop or are barely moving. It's always possible that your competitors are sailing at full speed and making a large gain. We could lose one hundred percent of our lead in two hours.

As it turns out we were caught between two wind systems. The new wind was coming out of the north and the wind that we had sailed the entire race in was generally out of the southeast. Often when two competing winds collide, there is no wind during the transitional period. This can last from ten minutes to three hours. The good news is that the transition only took a half hour and as the northwest breeze filled in, we quickly dropped our wind seeker and put up our big #1 genoa.

We were now approximately 58 miles from the finish line and it looked like we would be beating for the rest of the race. As we sailed upwind at a speed of four knots, the bigger boats quickly sailed up to us and *Epic* and *Sagitta* were sailing away. We could barely see them. We knew this was not *Bernida's* strongest point of sail, but we had a big lead in our class and believed we could hang on to the finish. By 7:30PM Sunday evening, we were off Rogers City and making steady progress towards the island.

We were having lots of fun crossing tacks with NA40's, C&C 41's and a very well sailed Peterson 43, *Blitz*. Gradually these boats sailed off the horizon and we could not see any boats in front of us or behind us. We figured the boats in our class must have gotten caught in the same transitional wind that we did and were not able to make up any distance on us.

In addition to his role as race chairman, Greg Thomas was also racing his 43' boat, *Pendragon* on the Shore Course. Once they got far enough North within range of cell phone towers, Greg checked to see how far *Bernida* was behind *Pendragon*. Although he expected *Bernida* to be 20 miles behind them, she was only one mile back. The entire *Pendragon* crew was excited to hear the news about *Bernida* from Greg.

Around midnight, the wind had picked up to eighteen knots and the waves were building. The conditions were alarming. Each time Bernida would slam into a wave, we wondered what would break. During the race, a hairline crack had opened up in the aft part of the deck at the back of the cockpit. In the lighter winds you could only stick a dime in the crack and it did not appear to be getting any bigger. After an hour of pushing Bernida to the limit however, this crack had opened up to the point where Connor said, "Mr. Declercq, I can stick my fingers through this crack in the deck." We suspected we would never make it to the finish line if we could not take some load off the boat. The combination of the loads from the running backstay and main sheet were tearing the aft quarter of the boat off. We made the decision to drop our big genoa and switch to the #3 jib.

Matthew was off watch while his dad was on the bow making the sail change. These sail changes were always difficult because the area of the bow was very small and there were no lifelines. They had to use hanks to attach jibs. A big wave came over the bow. Matthew heard a loud gasp out of his dad. He feared his dad had gone overboard! He leapt out of the cabin and saw that Al was holding onto the forestay. He had been hit by a wave and swallowed a lot of water. He had his harness on and it was obvious that he could not catch his breath. Because the dads had a rule that the sons were not allowed forward of the mast at night, Al declined Matthew's offer of assistance. Ward came forward and helped complete the sail change.

With the big genoa up, we were sailing at 6 knots. Once we had completed the change, we had reduced our speed to 4.5 knots. The crack in the deck had closed back up. We quit taking on water and Bernida had a much nicer motion through the water. As you can imagine, none of us wanted to reduce our speed but, you can't win a race if you don't finish and we believed sailing conservatively for a while would give us the best chance of finishing. We spent two hours questioning this decision.

By 2:00AM on Monday morning, the wind began to drop and we switched back to our big genoa. Bernida had weathered the big breeze and seas and we were back sailing in perfect conditions for her. The wind continued to drop to 3 knots. Getting up to the straits on Sunday night, Ward saw the Northern Lights (Aurora Borealis). Although, he had seen them before, they were never like this. We saw many shooting colors. The light show was incredibly beautiful! He had a hard time driving the boat upwind while trying to watch the light show. I thought about replacing Ward on the helm but soon realized that I would be just as distracted by the Northern Lights as Ward. Ward, Connor and I continued to enjoy the light show on our watch until a haze set in.

We were now off of the eastern corner of Boise Blanc Island at 4:30AM Monday morning. The wind was only 3 knots out of a direction of 312 degrees. With 9 miles to the finish line, we were on a pace to shatter Bernida's two previous elapsed times to the Island and it looked like we would win our class and be first overall. Not bad for a ninety one year old boat.

Sailboat racing, however, is never that easy. Soon we found ourselves becalmed. Our GPS was reading double zeros for speed and our ETA said "eternity". This must have been some Garmin (the GPS manufacturer) programmer's idea of a joke. We put our wind seeker up and looked for any whisper of wind we could find. The wind seeker can be a very effective sail in these conditions. At night, when you can't tell if you are on port

Northern Lights in the Straits of Mackinac—Photo by Gary Gee.

or starboard tack or beating or running, the wind seeker can be an excellent indicator. As the wind filled in, the crew could see that the wind was on our port beam and we set the main accordingly. Gradually the boat began to accelerate and we were moving at a full knot. At this rate we would finish at 2:00PM. The fastest boat on the Shore course, a Melges 32 named Bad Fish had finished and we needed to finish by 11:15 to win overall. We struggled for hours, trying to knock off a few miles. The southerly wind had pushed back north as it typically does as the sun heats up and we were back in the transition zone. Sometimes we were going 3 knots and sometimes we were only going a half a knot. As time went on it was appearing less likely that we would finish in time to beat Bad Fish.

Gradually the breeze built out of the south and we were sailing at 3 knots. We were three and a half miles from the finish

Three Miles From the Finish Line—Photo by Sara Declercq.

line and had to finish in an hour to become the overall winner of the race. As we looked to the south we could see the NA 40, Velero moving faster than us, closer to shore.

In a few minutes they moved forward on us ten degrees. Clearly there was more wind closer to shore. We were aiming at the finish line, sailing under our A-3 Asymmetrical spinnaker at a speed of 3 knots. We had been battling two Beneteau 36.7's for close to an hour. Ken suggested that we needed to abandon aiming at the finish line and change course to get closer to shore. Another couple minutes went by and the boats inshore were still moving faster than us. Ken said we are going to lose this race if we keep doing what we were doing and that we needed to get into the stronger wind. At Ken's insistence, we dropped our Asymmetrical spinnaker and put up our big genoa. We headed up thirty degrees and started to converge with the shore. The closer we got to the shore, the harder the wind was blowing. Each time I would begin to bare off and sail closer to the course, Ken would adamantly insist they we keep converging with the shore. Even though it took Bernida about forty degrees off the rhumb line, it was the right decision.

Sara stayed up all night tracking the boat. She had too much adrenalin going to fall asleep. At some times, it appeared the guys would finish during the night. On Monday morning at around 9:00AM, Sara called Roxanne to tell her that *Bernida* was about three miles from the finish line and to hurry down to the dock because they were going on a boat out to watch the guys finish. About three miles from the finish line, there were their husbands and their sons, slowly sailing to the finish on a very slight breeze. It was a great moment for the people on both boats. Roxanne was so relieved and thought to herself, "Another one done." Sara said she was messaging photos to her mom and dad and to Allison in Europe so they could see the boat sailing to the finish line. It was a very proud moment for her to watch Matthew helm the boat across the finish line and capture the win!

My dad, Maury Declercq, was a legendary sailor. The old timers will tell you that he understood what it took to win a Mackinac Race perhaps better than anyone. Maury passed away ten years ago and his ashes have been living in my closet since then. He had requested that his ashes be spread in the Straits of Mackinac. For one reason or another, neither my brother nor I ever got around to honoring his wish. On Saturday morning, as I was packing for the race, my eyes focused on the box that contained my dad's ashes. It felt good to be with my dad that morning and it occurred to me at that moment that he might just want to win one more

Mackinac Race. So I picked up the container and put him into a waterproof backpack. When we arrived at Bernida, I carefully stored Maury on a hook forward of the mast. Sara and Matthew were the only ones that I told that I had brought him along. Just knowing he was on board was an inspiration for me. I really wanted to win the race for him. I suspect he felt the same way about wanting to win on my brothers' and my first Mackinac race 45 years earlier. We were just twelve at the time. Approximately a mile from the finish line, I was driving and Ken was flying the spinnaker. I asked Matthew to go below and get his grandfather. The crew was a bit bewildered. They did not know that my dad, Maury, was on board. Matthew came on deck with the backpack and took over the helm. I removed Maury from the pack and told the crew about his wish. As we were nearing the finish line, I opened the container and began to pour his ashes into the lake. The crew was very quiet and it was a magical feeling, getting to win one more race with my dad while honoring his request and being able to share this moment with my son. Life doesn't get any better than this.

  Once we were into the better breeze, we switched back to our asymmetrical and paralleled the shoreline all the way to the finish line. Thank goodness for Ken's insistence that we get closer to the shore for the better breeze. Insistence might be too nice a word to describe the dialog. One of the many reasons that I love sailing with Ken is his competitive nature and passion. Thank God he brought his "A" game on this race.

  We sailed a longer distance, but our extra boat speed more than made up for it and we beat the two Beneteau's that we had been dueling with over the finish line by thirty minutes. This was a bold call that ended up ensuring that we would be first overall. We beat Bad Fish by 8 minutes. Bernida's record now stands;

Approaching the Finish Line. Photo by Sara Declercq.

Al Spreading his Dad's Ashes While Approaching the Finish Line. Photo by Sara Declercq.

three Mackinac races and three first place overall finishes!

In retrospect, Jeff Steiner, who wrote the song, "Sail On For Me My *Bernida*," feels that "gold stars" should go to Toby Murray for finding her, to Bart Huthwaite for buying her, to Emory Barnwell for restoring her and to Al Declercq for racing her.

Prior to the race, Jeff hoped for moderate weather that would enable the boat to stay together over such a long distance. He knew they had a very experienced crew and hoped there would be no major equipment failures. After many years on the waiting list to become a member of the Mackinac Island Yacht Club, he was made a member. During the race, he and

Bernida

Bernida Crossing the Finish line (Note Smoke From Cannon). Photo by Marcin Chomiecki.

his family stayed at the Yacht Club watching the race through Bayview's internet monitoring system. He was stunned with each update as *Bernida* maintained her lead throughout the race. He really didn't think it could win, but would be happy if it could finish. He had a power boat ready to go out and greet the guys as they approached the island. Sara and Roxanne joined him on the boat. They threw them a tow line after crossing the finish line and towed them into the harbor.

To everyone's surprise, they received a standing ovation from all the sailors who had finished ahead of them. The boats that finished ahead of them were mainly the larger boats that sailed on the Cove Island course. The huge reception gave Jeff goose bumps and he became very emotional. It was the perfect ending to a perfect race.

This was my 45th Port Huron to Mackinac Race and easily the most memorable. To have an opportunity to sail with two of my best friends and our three sons on the boat that won the first

Bernida

*Tow into Mackinac State Dock.
Photo by Jeff Steiner.*

*Arrival at Mackinac Island.
Photo by Marcin Chomiecki.*

Bernida

Mackinac Race is an indescribable feeling. I can't imagine that I will ever sail in another Mackinac race that was as rewarding as this one.

On Monday evening after *Bernida* had finished the race, Ted Everingham saw the entire *Bernida* crew with Sara and Roxanne at the Jockey Club restaurant. They were as excited as kids. He doesn't think Al was ever more excited than after this race. He felt that Al did it right and rigged the boat properly. Ted wrote a cover article for the June/July issue of Grosse Pointe Magazine featuring a photo of *Bernida*. While Ted was relating his memories of the whole *Bernida* story, he said, "I get excited all over about this."

Ted was asked to speak about *Bernida* at a press conference. Members of the press usually want to hear about the newest, biggest and fastest boats. Not this year, they wanted to hear about the oldest.

Bernida

OFFICIAL RESULTS
2012 Bell's Beer Bayview Mackinac Race
CLASS: PRHF "H"

Boat	Rating	Finish Time	Elapsed Time	Corrected	Rank
Bernida	192 / 0.8760	Mon-11:27:48	47:27:48	41:34:42	1
Wind Stalker	165 / 0.9091	Mon-13:18:17	49:18:17	44:49:20	2
Chippewa	174 / 0.8978	Mon-14:45:09	50:45:09	45:33:54	3
Camelot	153 / 0.9246	Mon-14:18:27	50:18:27	46:30:53	4
Zubenelgenubi	192 / 0.8760	Mon-19:04:40	55:04:40	48:14:55	5
Sea Wise	228 / 0.8355	Mon-21:59:39	57:59:39	48:27:09	6
Albacore	174 / 0.8978	Mon-18:01:19	54:01:19	48:30:01	7
Courage	168 / 0.9053	Mon-17:34:50	53:34:50	48:30:21	8
Wyle E. Coyote	177 / 0.8941	Mon-18:29:44	54:29:44	48:43:25	9
Sleeping Tiger	147 / 0.9326	Mon-16:19:59	52:19:59	48:48:14	10
Wavelength	147 / 0.9326	Mon-16:52:29	52:52:29	49:18:33	11
immisericors	147 / 0.9326	Mon-17:48:06	53:48:06	50:10:25	12
Nereus	147 / 0.9326	Mon-21:54:51	57:54:51	54:00:32	13
Alida	156 / 0.9207	Mon-22:43:15	58:43:15	54:03:47	14

Bernida

2012 OVERALL SHORE COURSE WINNER

DIVISION II - SHORE COURSE

Sail	Boat	Owner/ Skipper	Finish Time	Elapsed Time	Corrected	Class	Div.
USA 38	Bernida	Al Declercq	Mon-11:27:48	47:27:48	41:34:42	PHRF H	1
USA 115	BadFish	Bill Bollin	Mon-02:08:13	36:48:13	41:40:35	PHRF D	2
USA 50666	Jayhawker	Ken Brown	Mon-05:07:56	39:47:56	43:15:34	J120	3
USA 15370	Eliminator	Paul Van Tol	Mon-09:35:09	45:15:09	43:42:21	PHRF G	4
CAN 152	Irresistible too	Gerald Hines	Mon-06:22:00	41:02:00	44:36:05	J120	5

L to R: Fred, Ward, Connor, Ken, Al & Matthew.
Photo by Sara Declercq.

Roxanne really didn't realize what a big deal it was until she saw the reception in the harbor while towing *Bernida* to a boat slip. Sailors and bystanders everywhere were on their feet clapping and cheering for this historic feat.

In retrospect, she was glad the boat stayed in one piece. Only later did Connor tell her about the crack in the deck that was getting wider and wider under the strain of stronger winds Sunday night. Her ultimate conclusion about the race: "Someone was watching over them. They were very fortunate."

One hour after Greg Thomas arrived at the Mackinac Island Harbor aboard *Pendragon*, he saw *Bernida* being towed in. Like everyone else, he celebrated *Bernida*'s arrival and ran down to help the crew tie up at the dock. He feels that God gave them perfect conditions for the race. Going into the race he would have bet against them to finish and certainly to win.

Fred said, "It was one heck of an accomplishment. I'm glad we finished during the day." He thought they were the overall winner, but they had to find out later after it was official. The enthusiastic reception in the harbor and recognition by the fleet was unexpected and very much appreciated. He thought it was great fun to have a crew made up entirely of fathers and sons. As he summed it up, "It was a special summer. We took Al's vision and made it a reality."

Looking back on the race, Ward was surprised that the "thing held together." During test runs earlier in the summer, they loaded it up and tried to break it on Lake St. Clair with the wind blowing twenty knots. Nothing was breaking. Beating into the straits, however, the wind began building eight to ten to twelve knots and eventually eighteen knots. In his words, "Stuff that shouldn't move began moving. If there were any worse conditions, we would have been smoked."

Bernida

He believes that taking a ninety one year old racing boat, lost in a barn, and winning it again was a great achievement. Sailing with three fathers and sons made it special. He also saw that Matthew and Connor were becoming great offshore sailors in a short time. In the harbor, it was the coolest arrival at the end of the race. People were taking pictures and cheering for us. Reporters were conducting interviews. It was really nothing heroic, just a sailboat race.

Although Ward has been in hundreds of races, he said, "This was the most enjoyable one I ever raced. Barreling to Hawaii on a Transpac 52 was not as great as this!" Sara recalls he said to Matthew at dinner on Monday night, "I bet someday, thirty years from now, we will be here with our sons after racing, telling the *Bernida* story again and what we did with our dads."

Upon the race's successful conclusion, Barb Detwiler celebrated the amazing victory when talking to Fred, Ward, Sara and Roxanne. In her own words, "The whole experience was a great bonding opportunity for all."

Matthew was at the helm when *Bernida* went over the finish line. He drove the last ½ hour while just ghosting along from puff to puff. Once in the harbor, everybody who saw them started clapping and cheering. He never saw anything like it before. In his words, "They were waiting there for us to arrive and gave us a standing ovation." He didn't know until then that people were that hyped up about their accomplishment. He remembers that his mom was a little nervous, but she was also very excited about what they were doing. He was happy to see her on that power boat and able to be with them and watch them finish. He felt that the crew and the boat were ready to win. They couldn't have had better weather.

Like every person aboard *Bernida*, Ken was overwhelmed by

their reception in the harbor. The standing applause of their peers was the highest form of recognition. They had done the impossible.

Connor and his dad, Ken, have bonded over the years while sailing together. This particular race was quite emotional for both of them. One of Connor's comments was, "It's not every day a sixty year old can climb the mast of a racing boat underway." This was the seventh Bayview Mackinac Race with his dad. Without a doubt, this was his most memorable race and was a moment in time he'll have for the rest of his life. Although Roxanne, his mom, usually has pre-race jitters, she was even more worried about their safety on this race. In the end, however, she was on the boat to greet them three miles from the finish. He thought it was very special to see her out there providing such great support.

Emory Barnwell, who spent two years restoring the boat, was on the Island and aware that *Bernida* was leading the race with Al and his crew aboard. It created a big buzz among the townspeople on the Island who were tracking the boat as they came up Lake Huron. Emory tracked it online and his mom kept calling him to give him updates. She was very excited. Many other people on the Island were tuned into it as well. As *Bernida* began to approach the finish line, Emory got into a powerboat and followed her into the harbor. He went down to *Bernida*'s boat slip and met Al and his crew in the harbor once it arrived.

In Emory's own words: "It killed me that I couldn't get it in the water in 2011. It's pretty cool that I rebuilt a boat that could finish ahead of all these race boats. The weather conditions were ideal for that boat. It's kind of ironic the way it turned out." Emory has been working with Al for two years now. Al and

Bernida

Emory worked on other boats together, the sail maker and the boat builder.

The harbor greeting still gives Sara goose bumps. She never saw anything like it. She was crying and wanted to get off the powerboat and hug those guys. She couldn't get Matthew and Al in her arms fast enough. "My brother was there and I was on the phone with my mom and dad, who was in the car headed up to the Island. I stayed up all night waiting for them to arrive. I have met Al on the docks for the past 26 years and Matthew for the past 5 years. Many of those races, they have won. I don't know if any victory could be as exciting as this one! I could not be more proud of them or happier to be a part of this history." After the hugging was done, Matthew wanted to clean the boat and asked her if she would return to their room on the

L to R: Ken, Al, Matthew, Fred, Connor, Ward.
Photo by Sara Declercq.

Island and retrieve the mainsail cover and power cord. So, for Matthew, it was "back to the business at hand."

JULY 17TH MACKINAC RACE AWARDS PARTY
MACKINAC ISLAND

For the 2012 race the Mackinac awards party moved to a new location just down the hill from the Grand Hotel. For many years the party was held at Mission Point and we all wondered how this year's party would differ. This is easily one of the best sailing parties you can find anywhere in the world. Bayview Yacht Club does a great job with this event. I don't know why, but every year the sun is shining and the breeze is perfect for the temperature, regardless of the weather forecast or what the conditions are leading up to the party. Our crew was understandably suffering a little from the previous evening's celebration at Horn's as we passed through the party

L to R: Matthew, Al, Bob LaMere & Bill LaMere at Awards party. Photo by Sara Declercq.

Bernida

Sara Declercq With 1st Overall Flag. Photo by Marcin Chomiecki.

Al, Sara & Matthew Declercq. Photo by Marcin Chomiecki.

entrance gates. But, soon the party was packed and the Endless Summer Band began to play. They are a great party band and a Mackinac party tradition. The lead singer, Faith Marie, changes costumes for every set and each year has a surprise for the crowd. This year's host, the Grand Hotel, lived up to their reputation.

This is truly a first class company and a Michigan jewel. Our crew was joined at the party by, Roxanne Flaska, Sara Declercq and Sara's dad and uncle, Bob and Bill LaMere. Bob and Bill had been following Bernida on the website tracker and got so wound up that they decided to hop in the car and drive up to the Island. After all, Bob worked hard on getting the boat ready. He should have been there.

It was great they could join us for the celebration. It was such an incredible feeling when it came time to walk up the stairs to the stage and accept our award when Bernida was announced as the winner of Class "H". Once the class awards were over, we got to make a second trip to accept our Shore Course Overall flag.

The smiles on everyone's faces showed how excited we were to walk up on that stage again and from the noise of the crowd, it was obvious they were just as happy as we were to see Bernida take this overall win. Most of the competitor's conversation prior to the start of the race was about how far we would make it before we were forced to withdraw from the race. The over

Ken, Roxanne & Connor Flaska at Awards Party.
Photo by Sara Declercq.

Bernida

under was somewhere between Harbor Beach and Harrisville. Bernida proved to be up to the task, aided by favorable weather conditions.

Whole Bernida Family—Photo by Marcin Chomiecki.

Bernida

July 18th Round The Island Race Mackinac Island

This is a great race and a favorite of the local racers. The race starts near the east end of the Island and the fleet circles the Island counter-clockwise and finishes off the main break wall. Our crew consisted of Toby Murray, Bart Huthwaite, Jeff Steiner and his son Mitchell & daughter Kelsey and Matthew and Al Declercq. We met at the State dock around noon and boarded the boat. Matthew took charge and explained to everyone where things were on the boat, how things worked and how we were going to get out of the dock. Shortly afterwards we walked Bernida back out of the slip. As the crew shoved off, we hoisted the main and jib simultaneously. Bernida has a neutral helm while sailing, and requires a main and headsail to steer the boat straight. If you try to sail with the main only, Bernida is hard to keep from heading up into the wind. If you only have a jib up, Bernida's bow falls off and heads downwind. The balanced helm is fast because you are not using the rudder as a break while sailing, but it does make it difficult to maneuver in tight spaces.

With both sails hoisted, we began to sail out of the harbor. The looks on Bart's, Toby's, and Jeff's faces were priceless. They had worked so hard to restore Bernida and finally they were going to see how Bernida performs on the race course. I only wish that Emory had been able to join us. This was a perfect day for a race. The skies were clear and the sun was warm. The winds were out of the east at fifteen miles per hour. We were a little late for the start and rounded the first buoy in fourth place. We were able to bear off slightly at the first mark and

Start of Round The Island Race—Photo by Andre Dupre.

begin to rig the spinnaker in anticipation of being able to set it shortly. When we reached the eastern tip of Mackinac Island, we were able to bear off enough to set the spinnaker. I turned the helm over to Bart and we hoisted the spinnaker. This is Bernida's favorite point of sail and we quickly moved into third place.

We carried the spinnaker all the way down the back side of the Island and extended our lead on the fleet behind us. The two boats ahead of us, Natural High and Saint Barbara, were considerably bigger and faster boats. All we needed to do was finish less than twenty minutes behind them to win the race (on corrected time). When we reached the west end of the Island, we dropped the spinnaker and hoisted our jib.

We estimated that we were only seven minutes behind and felt good about our chances to win the race. Gradually we were able to head up towards the wind as we worked our way around the western end of the island until we were sailing hard on the wind. The lead boat had sailed a little too close to shore and the tree line was blocking their wind. We chose a route that was a couple hundred yards longer but were able to sail in a good breeze and closed the gap a little. This was fortunate for us because once the lead boats broke through the blanketed area; they began to stretch their lead at an alarming rate. We were able to hang on and finished fifteen minutes behind the lead boat to win the race! This completed a perfect season for Bernida.

  As we sailed back to Bart's mooring, I looked at Matthew and realized at that moment just how attached he had become to Bernida and knew he was really going to miss her. He had poured his heart into getting Bernida ready to race and loved her like a trusted pet. Although I did not have as strong of an attachment, I would miss Bernida as well. Bernida is an amazing boat and we had just completed a once in a lifetime journey. When we decided to purchase Bernida, we had high expectations. I have always been blessed, or cursed, with an inability to see anything other than a successful outcome. That being said, even an eternal optimist could not have envisioned how well the season and the resurrection of Bernida would turn out.

Indeed, Matthew had invested a lot of himself in all the weeks and months of his work on *Bernida*. He became very attached to the boat as most sailors do. While on the ferry back to the mainland, Matthew looked at *Bernida* moored in the harbor. He turned to his mom and said, "I don't want to let her go." She responded, "Neither do I, Matthew, neither do I. She's part of our family now."

Bernida

ROUND THE ISLAND RACE STARTS STRONG; BERNIDA TAKES TOP HONORS
By Matt Mikus, Mackinac Island Town Crier

The crew of *Bernida* accepts the prize for the Round the Island Race overall winner. *Bernida*, which also won in its division and class during the Bell's Beer Bayview Mackinac Yacht Race earlier in the week, was the first boat to win the race hosted by the Bayview Yacht Club in 1925. Pictured accepting the award are (from left) Kelsey Steiner, Jeff Steiner, race committee chairman David Rowe, Bart Huthwaite, Toby Murray, and Mitch Steiner. (Not pictured are Al and Matthew Declercq.) Thirteen ships competed in the Round the Island Yacht Race Wednesday, July 18, and *Bernida*, the first winner for the inaugural Bayview Mackinac Yacht Race in 1925, took the top honors overall with a corrected time of 1 hour, 28 minutes, and 39 seconds, followed by *Natural High*, and *Saint Barbara*.

Accepting Round The Island Race 1st Place Award. Photo by Matt Mikus of Mackinac Island Town Crier

Bernida

Donation of Bernida to the Michigan Maritime Museum, South haven, Michigan

Jim Spurr is a vice president of the board of the Michigan Maritime Museum (MMM) located in South Haven, Michigan and chairman of the *Bernida* Committee. He has been an attorney in Kalamazoo, Michigan with the law firm of Miller Canfield for thirty two years. He has been a sailor for thirty seven years and is actively involved in the preservation of Michigan maritime history. Jim is a firm believer that the *Bernida* saga is an important chapter in the state's maritime history.

When contacted by Jeff Steiner regarding the possible donation of *Bernida* to the MMM, Jim indicated that he would ask the board if it wanted to make a commitment at its August, 2012 meeting. The board decided to go ahead with the *Bernida* project. Although other Michigan museums were also interested, Jim felt that the MMM was uniquely qualified to become the preferred future home of *Bernida*. Jim and his wife were on the Island in July of 2012 for *Bernida*'s historic run. It was at the Mackinac Island Yacht Club that he met Toby, Bart, Al and Sara.

He told Jeff that the MMM was the only museum that had craftsmen who could maintain the boat at a high level of sea worthiness. He stated that the museum would keep *Bernida* in the water and apply for State of Michigan licensure in the spring of 2013. After identifying a captain suitable to the United States

Bernida

Coast Guard, the museum would offer daysails to the public for a fee. These outings would hopefully generate the funding needed to assure a sustainable future for the boat. The decision was made that the MMM would receive the boat after the 2012 Round the Island Race.

   Their arrangement, in concept, would allow for a newly formed not-for-profit entity, acceptable to MMM's insurance carrier, to charter the boat for the last three weeks of each July, provided the new entity could demonstrate the successful placement of an adequate insurance policy. During this time, the boat would be available on Mackinac Island in order to coincide with the Port Huron and Chicago Mackinac Races. Although, this is not a certainty at the time of writing this book, everyone involved is hopeful that it can become a reality.

MICHIGAN MARITIME MUSEUM PRESS RELEASE:

   The Michigan Maritime Museum of South Haven, Michigan, home of the tall ship, Friends Good Will and river launch, Lindy Lou, announces a significant addition to its collection of historic artifacts pertaining to Great Lakes maritime history: R 38, *Bernida*.

   Al Declercq, President of Doyle Sails, Inc. and most recent owner of the famed yacht *Bernida* generously gifted the champion to the Michigan Maritime Museum soon after crossing the finish line in the 2012 Bayview-Mackinac Race, winning the coveted first position in the "shore course." Declercq, skipper and one of three fathers of three sons aboard as crew, sailed *Bernida* to her third victory in that race – 87 years after *Bernida* crossed the same finish line in the inaugural race in 1925. In addition, just two years later *Bernida* was the overall winner again in 1927.

Declercq commented, "For a 91 year old boat to claim an overall victory twice in the same race, generations apart and against a much larger and more competitive fleet, is truly remarkable. Realizing her significance in yachting history, I and those involved in her restoration were impressed with the Michigan Maritime Museum's use of skilled volunteers who will not only lavish the care on her she deserves, but continue to sail her. It is the best possible future for any iconic sailboat."

Declercq explained, "It was always thought that if we could enter her in another Bayview-Mackinac Island race, her story would come around full circle. It would be interesting to see how a beautiful set of lines, well cut sails and experienced skipper and crew would fare against a state of the art racing fleet. Well, now we know…*Bernida* is none the slower for her age!"

The Michigan Maritime Museum has already launched the champion. As her planks swell from her brief time out of the water, the museum's volunteer crew turn their attention to her rig in preparation for a few trial sails yet this fall. Next summer, visitors to the museum will be able to experience what is the equivalent of a ride in a Duesenberg or a flight in a Sopwith Camel. Four passengers at a time, with a skipper and crew, will experience yachting history dating back to the early 1920's.

Executive Director Patti Montgomery explains, "The Michigan Maritime Museum is where visitors can not just read about maritime history or view objects of our maritime past, but where you can get out on the water and experience the sights, sounds and smells of a rich history spanning hundreds of years. *Bernida* is the perfect example of what was happening all over the Great Lakes in the early 20th Century." Jim Spurr, Vice President of the Museum and Chair of its "*Bernida* Committee"

Bernida

affirmed, "We marvel at the beauty and grace of her lines, the uncompromised performance, sophisticated engineering and the thrill of a graceful R Class yacht slicing through the water. She is the stuff of dreams for any true sailor. We are thankful to all of those whose vision saved an icon and for Mr. Declercq and his generosity."

The Michigan Maritime Museum is a not for profit organization located at the draw bridge in South Haven. For more information call 1-800-747-3810 or visit www.michiganmaritimemuseum.org. Source: News release and photo from Michigan Maritime Museum

Bernida

Bernida's New Home at the Michigan Maritime Museum.
Photo by Jim Spurr